THE AMAZING
WORLD CUP
COMPENDIUM

THE AMAZING
WORLD CUP
COMPENDIUM

NICK BROWNLEE

PORTICO

First published in the United Kingdom in 2010 by
Portico
10 Southcombe Street
London
W14 0RA

An imprint of Anova Books Company Ltd.

Copyright © 2010 Nick Brownlee

Illustrations by Gary Weston

The moral right of the author has been asserted.

ISBN 978 1 90603 294 4

Material in this title has previously appeared in *Motson's World Cup Extravaganza*.

A CIP catalogue record for this book is available from the British Library.

10 9 8 7 6 5 4 3 2 1

Printed and bound by WS Bookwell, Finland

This book can be ordered direct from the publisher at www.anovabooks.com

⚓ FOREWORD ⚓

When it was announced that South Africa was to host the 2010 World Cup finals – the first time the continent had ever been chosen to stage football's four-yearly jamboree – it was trumpeted as the moment football truly went global.

In truth, though, the World Cup has always lived up to its billing. Eighty years ago the very first finals were held in Uruguay, far from the game's spiritual home in Europe, and a place that in the days before air travel would have taken the best part of a month to get to by boat. Thirteen teams participated (of which only four made the long transatlantic journey from Europe), but nevertheless the foundations were laid for a competition that would ultimately become a glittering spectacle, the world's most popular sporting event.

The unprecedented global reach of the World Cup in the 21st century cannot be denied. In 1930, the first match between France and Mexico was watched by 1,000 fans. This year's opener in Johannesburg, between the hosts and, curiously, Mexico again will be watched by 90,000 in the Soccer City stadium and more than half a billion TV viewers.

The allure of the World Cup is, of course, the witnessing the world's best players competing against each other – and watching the stars of the future making a name for themselves on the world stage.

This book celebrates the players and the teams who have made their mark on the history of the game.

But the aim has also been to delve behind the headlines, shining a spotlight on those lesser-known characters and incidents that are as much a part of World Cup folklore as the superstars and the great matches.

And, as you will see, there have been plenty! I hope you enjoy reading about them as much as I enjoyed writing this book.

Nick Brownlee
Cumbria, February 2010

⚑ IN THE BEGINNING ⚑

The first World Cup match took place on a warm Sunday afternoon on 13 July 1930 in the Pocitos suburb of Montevideo, the capital city of Uruguay. Just over 1,000 people watched France's Lucien Laurent score the competition's first goal with a powerful shot after nineteen minutes, then saw the French romp to a convincing 4–1 victory over Mexico. This was despite the European team losing goalkeeper Alex Thepot after just 10 minutes having been kicked on the jaw. Captain of France that day was Alex Villaplane, who 14 years later would be executed by his fellow countrymen for collaborating with the Nazis.

⚑ PENALTY FIRST ⚑

The semi-final between France and West Germany in 1982 was the first world cup match to be decided by a penalty shoot-out. Alain Giresse, the French midfielder, stepped up to take the first kick – and was a relieved man when goalkeeper Harald Schumacher went the wrong way. Unfortunately for Giresse, the rest of his team-mates weren't so accurate, and France crashed out of the competition 5–4.

⚑ ON, AND VERY NEARLY OFF ⚑

The fastest yellow card given to a substitute in a World Cup finals match was to South Korea's Cha Doo-Ri, who was booked just 20 seconds after coming on in the match against Poland in 2002.

⚑ ONLY IN JAPAN ⚑

The Kobe stadium in Japan, used during the 2002 World Cup to stage matches in Group F among others, had a unique computer system used to control the length and growth-rate of the grass on the pitch.

⚑ BLACKOUT IN BANGLADESH ⚑

Such was the global allure of the 1998 World Cup, impoverished districts of Bangladesh had four nights of blackouts due to a surge in power consumption as millions of people tuned in to watch football coverage from France.

⚑ DREAM TEAM ⚑

In 2002 FIFA selected their World Cup 'dream team' made up of the best players of the previous 40 years. Each to their own, of course – but Rivelino and Gerd Muller would surely have something to say about the inclusion of talented but less prolific stars Roberto Baggio and Romario.

Goalkeeper: Lev Yashin (USSR)
Defenders: Franz Beckenbauer (GER), Paolo Maldini (ITA), Roberto Carlos (BRA)
Midfielders: Diego Maradona (ARG), Michel Platini (FRA), Zinedine Zidane (FRA), Roberto Baggio (ITA)
Forwards: Johan Cruyff (HOL), Pelé (BRA), Romario (BRA)

⚓ WORLD CUP DISPUTE ⚓

According to a 1998 survey, the 1998 World Cup was responsible for causing an increase in the number of domestic fights, divorces and wife batterings. In one instance, a woman in Bristol described how she had been punched by her husband following an argument about which match to watch on TV.

⚓ STRIPPERS, NOT STRIKERS ⚓

Not everyone goes football crazy when the World Cup comes around. A survey of 1,000 British women revealed that 21 per cent of them would prefer to go and see male strippers than watch football, while 6 per cent would try to renew an old relationship while their husband or partner was engrossed in the world's biggest soccer tournament.

⚓ DROWNING THEIR SORROWS ⚓

After seeing their side lose 3–0 to unfancied Morocco at the 1998 World Cup, around 8,000 travelling Scotland fans drowned their sorrows by drinking 125,000 litres of beer between them. Several bars in St Etienne had to close after the barrels ran dry.

⚓ IN THE NAME OF THE FATHER ⚓

Who needs the pub? FIFA granted German Evangelical churches the rights to screen all World Cup 2006 matches free of charge. 'Football is a vital part of life', said Bishop Wolfgang Huber of the Evangelical Church. Amen to that.

⚓ AN UNWELCOME RECORD ⚓

In 2002, Hakan Unsal of Turkey became the 100th player to be sent off during the World Cup finals.

⚓ THE MISSING 'V' ⚓

Milko Gaidarski (1970) and Petar Mikhtarski (1994) are the only two Bulgarian World Cup players out of 154 not to have the letter 'v' at the end of their names.

⚓ WORLD CUP MASCOTS ⚓

Tournament	Mascot	Description
England 1966	'World Cup Willie'	A lion wearing a Union Jack jersey.
Mexico 1970	'Juanito'	A Mexican boy wearing a sombrero.
West Germany 1974	'Tip and Tap'	Two boys in West German shirts.
Argentina 1978	'Gauchito'	A boy in a gaucho hat.
Spain 1982	'Naranjito'	A smiling orange.
Mexico 1986	'Pique'	A chilli pepper.
Italy 1990	'Ciao'	A figure made of coloured blocks.
USA 1994	'Striker'	A cartoon dog.
France 1998	'Footix'	A cockerel.
Japan/S. Korea 2002	'Kaz, Ato and Nik'	Three manga-style cartoon characters.
Germany 2006	'Goleo VI and Pille'	A large lion in a German football top, accompanied by his friend – a talking football.
South Africa 2010	'Zakumi'	A green-haired leopard.

World Cup Willie
England 1966

Juanito
Mexico 1970

Tip & Tap
West Germany 1974

Gauchito
Argentina 1978

Naranjito
Spain 1982

Pique
Mexico 1986

Ciao
Italy 1990

Striker
USA 1994

Footix
France 1998

Kaz, Ato & Nik
Korea/Japan 2002

Goleo VI & Pille
Germany 2006

⚓ MYANMAR MISERY ⚓

Myanmar, known as Burma until 1989, finished second in the 1968 Asian Cup. But their record in the World Cup is, well, non-existent. Between 1930 and 1938 they did not enter, while in 1950 they were invited to enter but withdrew. From 1954–90 they did not enter. In 1994 they entered but withdrew without playing a match. In 1998 they did not enter and in 2002 they were entered but once again withdrew. In 2006, FIFA's patience snapped and Myanmar were banned from even entering the tournament. In seventeen tournaments they are the only national side registered with FIFA not to play a single World Cup qualifier.

⚓ GREAT GAMES: FRANCE 1–1 BRAZIL ⚓
(4–3 AFTER PENALTIES), 1986

A quarter-final in Guadalajara in which a host of brilliant but ageing players realised that this could well be their last hurrah on the world stage and performed accordingly. Careca scored after 17 minutes for Brazil, but Platini levelled 4 minutes before half-time. In the shoot-out, Socrates, Platini and Cesar all missed as France scraped through 4–3. But in many ways the score was unimportant. What caught the eye were the likes of Socrates, Platini, Rocheteau, Zico and Junior playing out of their skins for the last time, and the overwhelming feeling among millions of viewers that, whatever the result, this was the end of a golden era of World Cup football.

⚓ HAVELANGE SPLASHES OUT ⚓

Joao Havelange, the former President of FIFA, was not much of a footballer by all accounts. However, as a young man he represented Brazil in swimming at the 1936 Berlin Olympics and in water polo at the 1952 Games in Helsinki.

⚓ RONALDO'S ILLNESS ⚓

Just what was wrong with Ronaldo before the 1998 World Cup final? It is a mystery which provided the major talking point of the tournament, even more than France's 3–0 win. The drama began on the day of the match when the prolific striker was sensationally left out of the starting eleven. The reason given was an unspecified illness – which began a frenzy of speculation about what had happened. Rumours varied from epileptic fits to poisoning. Then, with barely an hour to go before kick-off, Ronaldo was back in the team, creating even more gossip. Had his sponsors insisted that he played? Was he really ill in the first place? Was coach Mario Zagallo playing mind-games with the French? Ronaldo played, but was woefully out of sorts. He missed the sort of chances he would normally be expected to gobble up as France cruised to victory. Later Ronaldo explained that even he didn't know what was wrong with him, except that he felt 'bad'. Four years later he was back to his best, scoring both goals in Brazil's 2–0 final win over Germany. But the puzzle remains about 1998 and the illness that conveniently sidelined Brazil's most influential player on the eve of the World Cup final.

⚓ HELLO ZICO ⚓

Zico, one of the more extravagantly gifted Brazilian strikers of the 1970s and 1980s, ended his career with a lucrative contract in Japan. But rather than taking the money and running when he finished playing, Zico stayed on and has been credited with transforming Japan into a credible world footballing nation. In fact, he is now manager of the Japanese team which qualified for the 2006 World Cup – where they are drawn in the same group as Brazil.

⚓ ROBSON'S CHOICE ⚓

Often it is the fates and not the manager's selections which can make or break the fortunes of a team competing in the World Cup. So it was with England in 1986. Bobby Robson's men made a disastrous start to their Mexican campaign, losing to Portugal and scraping a goalless draw against little Morocco. In their final game they were up against Poland, and anything less than a draw would see them on the first flight back to Blighty. Robson's selections had been roundly criticised, but now fates stepped in. In the Morocco match, England lost both skipper Bryan Robson (dislocated collar bone) and midfielder Ray Wilkins (sent off).

Without what were assumed to be his two most influential players and with the shape of his team unbalanced, Robson was forced to play little Peter Beardsley as a foil for striker Gary Lineker. Right from the first whistle it was clear that here was a match made in heaven. Beardsley was instrumental in all three of Lineker's first-half goals and would go on to score himself in the next match, a convincing 3–0 win against Paraguay. Lineker scored two this time, putting him on course for a Golden Boot and England for a quarter-final spot – neither of which seemed possible before the fates robbed Robson of his captain and his midfield general.

⚓ SAME COUNTRY, DIFFERENT NAME ⚓

Look back through the World Cup annals and there are a number of teams who have appeared in qualifiers and the finals who at first glance seem to have disappeared off the map. That's because, whether because of political or social change, they have changed their names to reappear with a new name. These countries include:

- **Benin** who as Dahomey attempted to qualify 1974
- **Burkina Faso** were known as Upper Volta in 1978
- **Democratic Republic of Congo** appeared as Zaire from 1970 to 1998
- **Czech Republic and Slovakia** were together Czechoslovakia from 1934 until 1994. They split in 1993 and completed the 1994 qualifiers as RCS - Representation of Czechs and Slovaks
- **Germany** were also known as Saarland in 1954 and German Democratic Republic, or West Germany from 1958 until 1990 before uniting back again
- **Indonesia** made a fleeting appearance in the finals as Dutch East Indies as 1938
- **Republic of Ireland** attempted to qualify as Irish Free States in 1934 and 1938
- **Israel** were known as Palestine in 1934 and 1938
- **Myanmar** was Burma in 1950
- **Netherlands Antilles** were Curaçao in 1958
- **Russia and Ukraine** were the USSR from 1958 until 1994
- **Serbia and Montenegro** were known as the Kingdom of Serbia and Montenegro in 1930
- **Sri Lanka** made a bid for World Cup glory as Ceylon in 1974
- **Surinam** were Dutch Guyana in 1938, 1962, 1966, 1970, and 1974
- **Vietnam SR** entered as South Vietnam in 1974 and 1978
- **Yemen** entered as both North Yemen and South Yemen in 1986 and 1990
- **Zimbabwe** entered as Rhodesia in 1970

⚐ REFUSED ENTRY ⚐

FIFA may give the impression that any nation can enter the World Cup, but in fact they have refused entry to sixteen teams since the tournament began in 1930. In all, 77 countries have withdrawn, been disqualified, suspended, excluded or expelled in seventeen World Cups.

The teams to be refused entry are:

Albania	–	1970
Belize	–	1990
Bolivia	–	1954
French Congo (Congo)	–	1966
Zaire (Democratic Republic of Congo)	–	1970
Costa Rica	–	1954
Cuba	–	1954 & 1970
Ethiopia	–	1957
Guatemala	–	1966
Guinea	–	1970
Iceland	–	1954
Korean Republic	–	1958
Mauritius	–	1990
Mozambique	–	1990
Spain	–	1938
Vietnam SR	–	1954

⚐ SECOND CHANCE SPURNED ⚐

Sierra Leone lost to Burundi in the first qualifying round of the 1958 World Cup and were therefore eliminated from the competition. Then war broke out in Burundi, which meant they had no choice but to withdraw. FIFA decided that Sierra Leone should therefore be reinstated, but domestic problems meant that they couldn't fulfil their fixtures. They therefore became the only country to be eliminated twice from the same World Cup.

⚓ THE WORLD OF FIFA ⚓

Six governing bodies make up the Federation of International Football Associations (FIFA). They are:

UEFA (Union of European Football Associations)
CAF (Confederation of African Football)
CONCACAF (Confederation of North, Central American and Caribbean Association Football)
CONMEBOL (Confederation of South American Football)
OFC (Oceania Football Confederation)
AFC (Asian Football Confederation)

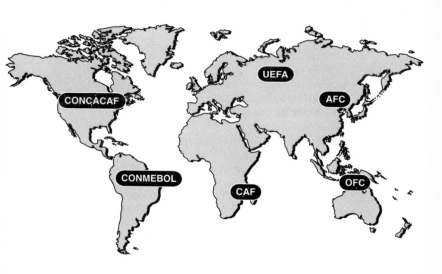

⚓ A GLOBAL MEDIA EVENT ⚓

About 3,700 journalists and 5,000 TV and radio crew were at the last World Cup. The company contracted to provide television coverage delivered 41,000 hours of pictures from 260 cameras and ten outside broadcast units, and 1.1 billion people tuned in to the final. However, there is a cost – the 2010 event is expected to generate a carbon footprint of 2.75 million tonnes – 9 times more than the previous finals in Germany, mostly because of international flights to South Africa.

⚓ BEER AND CHEER ⚓

Around half of the UK's 60,000 pubs will be tuning into the World Cup, and an estimated six million people are expected to watch England's matches. In Japan & South Korea 2002, despite the fact that England's matches kicked off early in the morning, the average number of pints sold soared from 18 million a day to 25 million. That means that each time England played it was worth an extra £20 million to the brewing industry.

⚓ SOUTH AFRICA 2010 ⚓

In 2010, South Africa will become the 16th nation to host a World Cup finals and the first from the African continent. Although historically the venue for the finals alternates between Latin America and Europe, in 1994 they were held in the USA, and in 2002 in South Korea and Japan. The decision to give the 2010 tournament to South Africa is part of FIFA's aim to open the game out to the rest of the world, as well as recognising the increasing development of sides like Cameroon and Nigeria. Five African nations – South Africa, Libya, Egypt, Tunisia and Morocco – put their names forward. Tunisia subsequently withdrew their bid when it was made clear that they would not be allowed to co-host with Libya (who had already narrowed their chances by saying they would refuse to let Israel compete if they won). On 15 May 2004, FIFA's Executive Committee voted in Zürich by 14 votes to 10 to award the finals to South Africa over Morocco. Egypt received no votes.

⚓ FRENCH FANCY ⚓

The 1998 World Cup final between France and Brazil was the first ever to be contested between the hosts and the defending world champions.

⚑ THIRD PLACE MONOPOLY ⚑

The clash between Holland and Croatia in 1998, which the Croatians won 2–1, was the fifth successive time that the third-place play-off had been contested by two European teams. Sweden beat Bulgaria 4–0 in 1994, Italy defeated England 2–1 in 1990, France beat Belgium 4–2 in 1986 and Poland defeated France 3–2 in 1982.

⚑ SENEGAL STUNNER ⚑

As World Cup shocks go, this one was seismic. The first game of the 2002 World Cup pitched reigning champions France against the unknowns of Senegal. Unknown, that is, until the 29th minute when, following a cross by El Hadji Diouf, midfielder Papa Bouba Diop forced the ball into the back of the net from close range. France, with the likes of Thierry Henry and Marcel Desailly in their team, were lousy and never looked like equalising. In fact, they failed to perform in their other games and went out in the group stage without scoring a goal. Senegal, in their first ever World Cup finals, remained sanguine about their sensational win. 'Before the game we all believe we can make a good result,' said midfielder Salif Diao. 'We won the game because we played better.'

⚑ NAREY WILL WE SEE THE LIKE AGAIN ⚑

In 1982, Brazil produced some sumptuous long-range goals that even today take the breath away. But ironically one of the very best goals of the competition was scored against Brazil and, of all people, by a Scotland defender. Just eighteen minutes had gone of the Group 6 match in Seville when David Narey received the ball midway inside the Brazil half, ran forward and then unleashed a simply unstoppable shot which flew into the net past the helpless Waldir Peres. It was a goal which stunned the Brazilians for precisely fifteen minutes, until Zico equalised. Three more goals followed as Scotland collapsed.

⚏ THE ART OF BEING A STRIKER ⚏

'The big thing is, everybody says it's being in the right place at the right time. But it's more than that, it's being in the right place all the time. Because if I make twenty runs to the near post and each time I lose my defender, and nineteen times the ball goes over my head or behind me – then one time I'm three yards out, the ball comes to the right place and I tap it in – then people say, right place, right time. And I was there all the time.' – England's Gary Lineker, winner of the Golden Boot in 1986

⚏ DEFENCE THE BEST FORM OF ATTACK ⚏

In 1990 Cameroon delighted the world with their plucky displays of attacking football, and very nearly went all the way to the semi-final. In the euphoria it was easy to forget that, when required, the Africans could be brutally pragmatic. In their opening match against Argentina they won the game 1–0, but also perpetrated one of the most cynical and over-the-top fouls ever seen in World Cup history in order to preserve their lead. With just a few minutes to go, Claudio Caniggia, Argentina's rangy, long-haired centre-forward burst clear from half-way and set off towards goal. Almost immediately one of the Cameroon defenders raced in with a challenge which, had Caniggia not somehow hurdled it, would have surely broken his legs. Still bearing down on goal, Caniggia was finally felled by Benjamin Massing, who executed a waist-high flying body check which almost knocked the striker into the third row of the stand. Needless to say Massing was sent for an early bath – the second Cameroon player to be sent off that day for fouls on Caniggia.

⚏ OPERA BUFFS ⚏

Wary of their reputation as global hooligans, FIFA decided to keep England fans as far away from the rest of Italia '90 as possible by confining them to the island of Sardinia for the first round of matches. In an effort to prove them wrong, a group of England fans made a point of soaking up the culture by going to see a performance of Verdi's opera *Aida* at a theatre in Cagliari. The verdict? 'Some nice tunes, but the intervals were too long!' one fan complained.

⚓ DINING IN REVERSE ⚓

In a bid to relieve the boredom between matches, in 1990 England's Terry Butcher and Chris Woods went to a restaurant in Cagliari with their smart Umbro tracksuits inside out. They then proceeded to order coffee, dessert, a main course and finished up with a starter. They must have been very bored indeed.

⚓ BELGIAN WOE ⚓

'The Goalposts Were English.' – Belgian headline after their agonising last-minute defeat by England at Italia '90

⚓ WISE WORDS ⚓

'There is no greater drama in sport than a soccer team trying to validate its national character in the World Cup.'
– US journalist Jeff Rusnak

⚓ WAR TALK ⚓

'Your mission is part of the confrontation between Iraq and the Forces of Evil embodied by the US and its allies.'
– *Al Qadissiya* newspaper of Baghdad on Iraq's 1994 World Cup qualification campaign

⚓ ONE SIDED ⚓

'Up to five goals is journalism. After that, it becomes statistics.'
– French reporter gives up after Sweden thrash Cuba 8-0 at the 1938 World Cup

⚓ BOMBED OUT ⚓

'God help them. Often I didn't know where the ball was going, so how could they?'
– 'Der Bomber' Gerd Muller offers words of sympathy to goalkeepers

⚓ FOOTBALL'S COMING HOME ⚓

'Home advantange is a double-edged sword; the crowd can either roar you on, or you can crumble beneath their too-great desire, the weight of it on your shoulders. But England didn't crumble in 1966, and 103 years after the FA was founded in the Freemasons' Tavern in Lincoln's Inn Fields, the 8th World Cup was played on the grounds of the world's first soccer clubs, and won and brought home by the people who made them.'– editorial in *The Times* after England won the 1966 World Cup final.

⚓ IT'S A LINEKER! ⚓

During Beirut hostage John McCarthy's captivity, Gary Lineker scored six goals for England at Mexico '86. According to McCarthy, who was allowed to listen to coverage on the radio while chained to a radiator, this led him for a while to think 'Lineker' was Arabic for 'goal'.

⚓ KEANE US MCCARTHY ⚓

Irish eyes weren't smiling in the build-up to the 2002 World Cup following the mother of all rows between the Republic's manager Mick McCarthy and his star player and captain Roy Keane. Annoyed by what he regarded as sub-standard training facilities, Keane's frustration boiled over at a team meeting on the eve of their first game. Most of what was said is unprintable, but the gist was that Keane did not regard McCarthy as a good manager. McCarthy reacted by sending Keane home. Despite a concerted campaign to have him reinstated, in which even the Taoiseach (Prime Minister) Bertie Ahern tried to mediate, Keane did not play for Ireland again under McCarthy. Indeed McCarthy stated publicly that if Keane returned he would quit.

⚓ ANIMALS ⚓

'We have still to produce our best, and this is not possible until we meet the right sort of opponents, and that is a team that comes out to play football and not to act as animals.'
– Alf Ramsey after the infamous 1966 clash between England and Argentina

⚲ A–Z OF WORLD CUP GREATS ⚲

ADEMIR (Brazil, b. 1922 d. 1998): Considered one of Brazil's greatest ever strikers, and a precursor to such legends as Pelé and Zico, Ademir scored nine goals as the host nation blazed its way through the 1950 finals, hitting four in a 7–1 win over third-placed Sweden and two in a 6–1 demolition of Spain in the final group phase.

Tournaments: 1950
Games: 6
Goals: 9

BECKENBAUER, FRANZ (West Germany, b. 1945): Known universally as *der Kaiser* because of his elegant style and leadership qualities, Beckenbauer virtually invented the art of creative defending, maturing from a solid midfielder to an attacking sweeper in a long and illustrious career. He played in three World Cups, losing to England in 1966, enduring a frustrating shoulder injury in 1970, and finally, as captain, lifting the trophy on home soil in 1974. Later he would become coach of the national side, leading them to the final in 1986 and becoming the second man, after Mario Zagallo, to both play in and coach a World Cup-winning team in 1990. He recently headed the bid to have Germany selected as hosts of the 2006 World Cup, and is head of the organising committee.

Tournaments: 1966, 1970, 1974
Games: 18
Goals: 5

CUBILLAS, TEOFILO (Peru, b. 1949): One of the most prolific goalscorers in World Cup history, Teofilo Cubillas's ten goals were all the more remarkable considering they were scored in two tournaments eight years apart, and for a team which were generally considered rank outsiders but consistently rewrote the form book. His first tournament was in 1970 when he bagged five goals and helped Peru to the quarter-finals. In 1978, he scored five more – including two against Scotland – which propelled his side to the second stage. Cubillas was back, aged 32, in 1982, but age and a poor side were against him and he failed to score.

Tournaments: 1970, 1978, 1982
Games: 13
Goals: 10

DUNGA (Brazil, b. 1963): Never as flamboyant as his team-mates, Dunga was nevertheless the mainstay of three Brazil World Cup sides, and skippered the side which won the 1994 World Cup and reached the final in 1998. An excellent defensive midfielder, he brought much-needed solidity to sides full of gifted attacking individuals such as Romario, Ronaldo and Ronaldinho. Although not a noted goalscorer, Dunga bagged the penalty which secured victory in the 1994 shoot-out. Unfortunately, his nickname means 'Dopey' in Portuguese.

Tournaments: 1990, 1994, 1998
Games: 18
Goals: 0 (2 in penalty shoot-outs)

EUSEBIO (Portugal, b. 1942): You don't have to be a World Cup winner to be a World Cup star. Eusebio – known as the Black Pearl – dominated the 1966 finals in England, scoring nine goals and inspiring his unfancied Portugal side to a semi-final against the hosts. In the first group stage, he single-handedly tore apart Brazil, scoring twice to eliminate the 1958 and 1962 champions. Against North Korea, he rescued his team from 3–0 down by scoring four times. He was so popular in England that his waxwork was placed in Madame Tussauds – but it would be the last World Cup Eusebio would appear in, as Portugal failed to qualify for the finals again until 1986.

Tournaments: 1966
Games: 6
Goals: 9

FONTAINE, JUSTE (France, b. 1933): The first of a long line of mercurial French stars, Juste Fontaine combined artistry with clinical finishing in 1958 to claim the record for the most goals scored in a single tournament. His thirteen goals propelled France to the semi-finals, but it was in the third-place play-off against West Germany that Fontaine excelled himself by scoring four times in an emphatic win. Tragically, his career was cut short with a broken leg just two years later.

Tournaments: 1958
Games: 6
Goals: 13

GARRINCHA (Brazil, b. 1933 d. 1983): Manoel dos Santos Francisco was born a cripple, and as a child underwent a series of operations which left his left leg permanently twisted. Nevertheless, Garrincha ('Little Bird') became a footballing legend, a World Cup winner in 1958 and 1962 and a rival to Pelé for the title of greatest Brazilian footballer of all time. Defences were bamboozled by his dribbling, goalkeepers by his banana shot. The 1966 defeat against Hungary was not only his last game but the only time he had ever appeared on a losing side for Brazil. Sadly, off the pitch his personal life was a mess of marital and financial problems. He died of alcohol poisoning, impoverished and largely forgotten, in 1983 at the age of 49.

Tournaments: 1958, 1962, 1966
Games: 12
Goals: 5

HURST, GEOFF (England, b. 1941): Hurst earns his place in the legends list simply because of his exploits on that hot July day in 1966 when he scored the first – and so far only – hat-trick in a World Cup final. A late replacement for the injured Jimmy Greaves, Hurst grabbed his opportunity with both hands. He scored the vital goal against Argentina in the quarter-final then let rip in the final against West Germany. His third goal, rifled in from the edge of the penalty area, remains an iconic image of England's greatest tournament.

Tournaments: 1966, 1970
Games: 6
Goals: 5

JAIRZINHO (Brazil, b. 1944): Another Brazilian graces the list of legends. Jairzinho played in three tournaments between 1966 and 1974, but like so many of his team-mates he was at his bewitching best in Mexico 1970. Despite breaking a leg the previous season, he returned on top form and became the only player to score in every match including the final (Ghiggia of Uruguay scored in every round in 1950, but Uruguay only played 4 games.). His seven goals amounted to a masterclass in the finisher's art, ranging from long-range thunderbolts to delicate chip-ins. In fact his only dodgy goal was the 71st-minute mis-kick that put Brazil 3–1 ahead in the final. Although he failed to reproduce his best form in 1974, Jairzinho continued as a mainstay of the Brazil side, eventually winning his 80th and final cap in 1982 when he was 38 years old.

Tournaments: 1966, 1970, 1974
Games: 16
Goals: 9

KOCSIS, SANDOR (Hungary, b. 1929 d. 1978): Top scorer in the 1954 tournament with eleven goals, Kocsis was a phenomenal header of the ball and earned the soubriquet 'The Man with the Golden Head'. Alongside Puskas he was part of the magical Hungary side that laid waste to all before them prior to the World Cup, scored 24 goals in four matches in the tournament, yet choked spectacularly to lose in the final to Germany. Who knows what Hungary might have achieved had the country not been invaded by the Soviet Union in 1956. By the time the 1958 finals came around, Kocsis was playing in Spain and decided not to risk returning home. He retired in 1966 aged 37 and died in 1978 at the shockingly young age of 49.

Tournaments: 1954
Games: 5
Goals: 11

LATO, GRZEGORZ (Poland, b. 1950): Lato's hair might have visibly thinned over the course of three World Cup tournaments, but his appetite for the game remained throughout. He began in 1974 as a speedy right-winger, but his all-round game impressed almost as much as his goalscoring. That year he even overshadowed the prodigious Gerd Muller to become top scorer with seven. As the years passed and his speed diminished Lato amended his game accordingly and became even more influential. Although the Polish team misfired in 1978, in 1982 Lato and Zbigniew Boniek led the side to their second bronze medal in eight years.

Tournaments: 1974, 1978, 1982
Games: 20
Goals: 10

MARADONA, DIEGO (Argentina, b. 1960): Matthaus, Moore, Monti, Maier, Muller – all of them great players, but unfortunately for them there is only one 'M' when it comes to World Cup legends. Diego Armando Maradona's fans call him the greatest player ever, and even his detractors would argue that the only thing that keeps him behind Pelé in the pantheon is his disciplinary record. Quite simply, on his day Maradona was an unstoppable force, a whirlwind talent able to unpick the tightest defences and beat lesser teams virtually single-handed. Left out of the squad in 1978, Maradona erupted onto the world stage four years later, destroying Hungary with two goals, but was let down by an ageing side which lacked the teeth for a fight and were dumped out in the second group stage. In 1986 in Mexico, Maradona was on a stage all of his own. Forget the 'Hand of God', if you can. Think instead of the second goal against England, and the two against Belgium in the semi-final. Think of how Maradona's desire to win forced an average team to victory in the World Cup final. In 1990 he led his side to the final once again, but this time the West Germans got their revenge in an uninspiring match. Four years later, Maradona arrived in the USA determined to go out with a bang, but it was a tournament too far for a 34-year-old who had already developed a liking for the high life during his time playing in Spain and Italy. He lasted two games before being caught with the stimulant ephedrine in his system. His tournament and his World Cup career were over in one fell swoop. It was a sad end, but Maradona had already done enough for the good memories to eclipse the bad.

Tournaments: 1982, 1986, 1990, 1994
Games: 21
Goals: 8

NEESKENS, JOHANN (Holland, b. 1951): Neeskens was an integral member of the great Dutch side of the 1970s which transformed the way in which football was played, reached the World Cup finals of 1974 and 1978, yet won nothing and is therefore remembered as one of the great underachieving sides. Neeskens scored five goals in the 1974 tournament, including a sensational chip against Brazil and, of course, the penalty which gave Holland a second-minute lead in the final against West Germany. Although he didn't get on the scoresheet in 1978, he was again instrumental in guiding the Dutch to their second successive final.

Tournaments: 1974, 1978
Games: 13
Goals: 5

OVERATH, WOLFGANG (West Germany, b. 1943): Wolfgang Overath was a mainstay of the West German team for three World Cups and a supremely talented midfielder in his own right. He was a member of the 1966 side which lost to England in the final, but was undoubtedly at his best in 1970 when he was voted best midfielder of the tournament by the international media. He only scored three goals, but contented himself with being a ball-winner and a provider for the predatory West German front men. His international career was capped off in fine style as a member of the World Cup-winning side of 1974, which made him, along with Beckenbauer, one of the select band of players to have won gold, silver and bronze medals in World Cups.

Tournaments: 1966, 1970, 1974
Games: 19
Goals: 3

PELÉ (Brazil, b. 1940): What can you say? The only man to win three World Cup winners' medals, the youngest-ever winner of a World Cup, scorer of three goals in World Cup finals and twelve in all ... Pelé's list of achievements is part of World Cup folklore. Indeed in many ways Pelé *is* the World Cup. He was just seventeen when selected to play in the 1958 tournament. Many thought he was too young, but they were soon made to eat their words as the teenager stole the show with a goal in the quarter-final, a hat-trick in the semi-final and a brace in the final which included one of the greatest goals in World Cup history. In 1962 and 1966 his participation was curtailed through injury and brutish tackling, but in 1970 he returned in magisterial form, guiding a stellar team to World Cup success with a mixture of almost casual brilliance and deadly finishing. As important as how he played was the manner in which he conducted himself on the pitch. Pelé believed passionately in sportsmanship and the pursuit of individual excellence, and was quick to congratulate those who demonstrated those qualities. After beating England 1–0, the first person he sought out to swap shirts with was Bobby Moore, who had played the best game of his illustrious career that sweltering day in Leon. Although he retired from international football more than 35 years ago, Pelé remains a legend in the game.

Tournaments: 1958, 1962, 1966, 1970
Games: 14
Goals: 12

RUMMENIGGE, KARL-HEINZ (West Germany, b. 1955): It was always going to be a tough job following the likes of Helmut Rahn, Uwe Seeler and Gerd Muller as the leader of the West German front line, but Karl-Heinz Rummenigge not only scored goals but led the national side to two World Cup finals as captain, a worthy successor to Franz Beckenbauer. His first appearance was in 1978, where as the heir to Muller he acquitted himself well, scoring three goals in a misfiring team. In 1982 he was at the height of his powers, scoring five goals despite a rapidly deteriorating knee. There were those who said he should not have played in the final against Italy, but to many in the young German side Rummenigge was a figurehead. In the end it was Italy who won the Cup, not West Germany who lost it. In 1986, aged 31, Rummenigge was captain once again, and once again he led his side to the final despite being hampered by injury. His 95th and last international was the final against Argentina in which, typically, he scored a goal.

Tournaments: 1978, 1982, 1986
Games: 19
Goals: 9

SEELER, UWE (West Germany, b. 1936): Brought into the West German squad shortly after their 1954 tournament win, Uwe Seeler went on to play in four World Cups, scoring in every one, and captain his team in the 1966 final against England. His 21 appearances was a record only bettered in recent years by his fellow countryman Lothar Matthaus and Italy's Paolo Maldini. Short, stocky and powerful, Seeler was the blueprint for West German strikers in the 1960s and 1970s and his nine goals belied the chaos he was capable of creating in opposition penalty areas.

Tournaments: 1958, 1962, 1966, 1970
Games: 21
Goals: 9

TOMASZEWSKI, JAN (Poland, b. 1948): Dismissed as a clown by Brian Clough, Jan Tomaszewski was anything but. His heroics knocked England out of the 1974 World Cup at the qualifying stage, and his consistent brilliance between the sticks helped unfancied Poland to third place in West Germany. His forte was saving penalties. In 1974 he became the first goalkeeper to save two in the same tournament, denying Tapper of Sweden and Hoeness of West Germany. But his record of five clean sheets in eleven World Cup games stands alongside the very best in World Cup history.

Tournaments: 1974, 1978
Games: 11
Goals conceded: 8
Clean sheets: 5

VALDERRAMA, CARLOS (Colombia, b. 1961): Best known for his vast mane of yellow hair, Carlos Valderrama was also an inspirational captain and a midfielder reckoned at his prime to be the very best in South America. Known as 'El Pibe' (the kid), Valderrama was one of few players to have captained his country in three World Cups. Although Colombia as a whole flattered to deceive it was not for the want of trying on Valderrama's behalf. His biggest World Cup moment was when he dribbled past several players and delivered a pinpoint pass to team-mate Freddie Rincon, who scored the necessary equaliser three minutes into injury time against eventual winners West Germany in 1990. That goal meant Colombia qualified for the second round. In 1994 Colombia disappointed again, and were knocked out in the first round, while in France four years later, at the age of 37, Valderrama's efforts were once again in vain.

Tournaments: 1990, 1994, 1998
Games: 10
Goals: 1

WALTER, FRITZ (West Germany, b. 1920 d. 2002): Although the prime of his career was lost to World War II, at the age of 34 Fritz Walter led West Germany back into the international fold and to unexpected World Cup glory in Switzerland. Thrashed 8–3 by the unstoppable Hungarians in a group match, few gave the Germans a prayer when the two sides met again in the final. Yet despite being two goals down in the first 10 minutes, Walter's never-say-die approach inspired his team-mates (including brother Ottmar) to a famous comeback. In 1958, aged 38, he led the team once again in Sweden. This time even his efforts were in vain as the Germans went out in the semi-finals. Walter then retired, but in 1962 national manager Herberger made a concerted effort to persuade the 42-year-old to make one last effort in Chile. Wisely, Walter said no. His place in World Cup legend was already assured (he would also be voted into the German team of the century in 1999).

Tournaments: 1954, 1958
Games: 11
Goals: 3

YASHIN, LEV (USSR, b. 1929 d. 1990): The great Soviet goalkeeper Lev Yashin was not just a superbly agile shot-stopper, he was an innovator who, in his three World Cup tournaments, changed the face of goalkeeping and brought it into the modern age. Before Yashin, keepers were simply the last line of defence who rarely strayed from their own goal-line. Yashin changed all that. He would roam his penalty area like a caged tiger, regarding himself as a fifth outfield defender, a sweeper in effect. He preferred to punch the ball to safety rather than catch it, hoping to start a counter-attack from the speedy Soviet wingers. First-choice goalkeeper for thirteen years, Yashin inspired his team to a World Cup semi-final in 1966 when he was 37 and, to many observers, at his best. Certainly his fitness and longevity paved the way for the likes of Dino Zoff and Peter Shilton, who were still at the top of their games into their forties. Tragically, Yashin did not enjoy the best of health in retirement. In 1986 a knee injury led to the amputation of his leg – and just four years later, at the age of just 61, he died of complications following further surgery.

Tournaments: 1958, 1962, 1966
Games: 13
Goals conceded: 18
Clean sheets: 4

ZOFF, DINO (Italy, b. 1942): Another veteran goalkeeper on the roster of World Cup legends, the great Dino Zoff is the oldest player to win the World Cup and the only goalkeeper to captain a cup-winning side. A colossus at the heart of a parsimonious Italian defence, Zoff, at the age of 40, gave the likes of Bruno Conti and Marco Tardelli the confidence to operate as playmakers in the 1982 tournament. With Paolo Rossi poaching up front, Italy cruised to the title. Zoff first came to prominence in Italy's 1968 European Championship winning team, but was dropped for the 1970 World Cup. He returned in 1974 and kept goal throughout three tournaments, conceding just sixteen goals.

Tournaments: 1974, 1978, 1982
Games: 17
Goals conceded: 16
Clean sheets: 5

⚓ MONTEVIDEO NASTY ⚓

There is a whiff of controversy in every World Cup, some more pungent than others, and the inaugural finals of 1930 were no exception. Indeed the competition in Uruguay was only two days old when all hell broke loose. Having comfortably won their first tie 4–1 against Mexico – the first ever World Cup match – France were drawn against Argentina, and found themselves right in the middle of a bitter South American feud. Problems began before the game, when the Argentine supporters, having arrived in ten boats, were brusquely searched for weapons by the Uruguayan police. With tensions running high, and the Uruguayans supporting the French, there were disturbances inside the ground when France had a man sent off and Argentina took the lead with just nine minutes remaining. But this was nothing compared with the mayhem that ensued three minutes later when the French player Marcel Langiller raced the length of the pitch and seemed certain to score, only for the Brazilian referee to blow for full-time. The pitch was invaded, and order was only restored when the referee – under advice from his linesman – realised his error. It was to no avail, however, as Argentina held out to win the game, prompting another pitch invasion and very nearly a diplomatic incident as the Argentine delegation threatened to quit the competition and go home.

⚓ BLOOD AND GUTS ⚓

One of the bloodiest encounters in World Cup history took place in the 1938 finals in France when Brazil and Czechoslovakia met each other in a first round clash in Bordeaux. From the outset, both teams set about each other with gusto bordering on violence. Brazil's Procopio was sent off for an unprovoked assault on Nejedly in the first half but, with the South Americans leading 1–0, things really kicked off after the interval. Riha and Machado became embroiled in a punch-up and were dismissed, Nejedly was stretchered off with a broken leg and Czech goalkeeper Planicka suffered a broken arm. When the dust settled, the match ended with nineteen players on the pitch, all but two of them having suffered some sort of injury. The match also finished 1–1, which meant the intriguing prospect of a replay. Fortunately this passed off without incident – mainly due to the fact that Brazil fielded nine new players and Czechoslovakia six. The Brazilians won the replay 2–1.

⚓ BRAVE SINDELAR ⚓

An added bonus for Germany following the annexation of Austria in 1938 was that they found themselves with the cream of Austria's national football side at their disposal. Indeed five Austrians played in the German team in that year's World Cup finals in France. One who refused to be assimilated was Mathias Sindelar, a stylish forward whose stance made him a national hero. But his defiance was no shallow gesture. Sindelar was devastated by the German invasion of his homeland, and a year later killed himself, unable to live under Hitler's rule.

⚓ NO FINAL ⚓

Uruguay were crowned World Cup winners in 1950 – although there was no final that year. Instead, FIFA and the host nation Brazil had devised a crackpot scheme in which the winners of four qualifying groups went into a final group. The winner of this group would be crowned champions. Any chance of the system working were dashed before the competition started, when only thirteen teams turned up. This meant that Uruguay were in a group that consisted of just themselves and Bolivia. Having dispatched their lowly South American rivals 8–0, the Uruguayans proceeded to the final group having played two games less than everyone else. Although Brazil gave them a run for their money, a 2–1 victory in the packed Maracana Stadium was enough to give Uruguay their second trophy in twenty years.

✠ GREAT GAMES: ITALY 4–3 WEST GERMANY, 1970 ✠

After a tight 90 minutes had ended 1–1, this all-European semi-final exploded in extra-time as the sapping Mexico heat forced errors from two solid defences. Having conceded a killer equaliser in the final minute, Italy went from bad to worse four minutes into extra time when Poletti and goalkeeper Albertosi got confused and allowed the predatory Gerd Muller to sneak in and score. Four minutes later, though, the Italians were back – this time from a German mistake. Held, normally a forward, got into a tangle in his own box following a Riva free-kick and Burgnich was on hand to smash the ball home from close range. The rollercoaster continued unabated as Riva put the Italians in front with a smart turn and shot, only for Muller to head the equaliser. Straight from the kick-off Boninsegna skinned the exhausted Schulz on the left and crossed for Rivera to calmly sidefoot the ball into the net. This fifth extra-time goal proved to be the last, and Italy were on their way to the final.

✠ THE BROTHERS CHANOV ✠

Brothers have been part of the same World Cup squad several times. But Victor and Vyacheslav Chanov are unique. They were in the 1982 Soviet Union squad, both as goalkeepers. However, neither of them played a match as the great Rinat Dassajev was first choice.

✠ NO SECOND CHANCE FOR THE CAPTAIN ✠

Captaining a winning side in the World Cup is a once-in-a-lifetime experience. But despite the best efforts of captains throughout history, none has done it twice. Diego Maradona captained Argentina to victory in 1986 and to a silver medal in 1990. Dunga of Brazil won as captain in 1994 and lost the final in 1998. Karl-Heinz Rummenigge is the only captain to lose two World Cup finals (1982 and 1986).

⚓ WE'LL BE BACK – AFTER THE WAR ⚓

Erik Nilsson of Sweden and Alfred Bickel of Switzerland are the only men to have played in the World Cup both before and after World War II. They both appeared in 1938 and 1950.

⚓ GOAL INCENTIVE ⚓

Winning the 1990 World Cup was not a realistic option for the United Arab Emirates, and sure enough they were knocked out after three straight defeats in the group stage. However, this was not for the want of trying – and indeed at times it seemed the entire team was intent on scoring a goal. The reason for their enthusiasm was revealed later. It turned out that whoever scored a goal would be rewarded with a Rolls-Royce. Khalid Ismael and Ali Juma'a duly scored the UAE's only goals and drove away from Italy with a smile on their faces.

⚓ PASSARELLA PREFERS REAL MEN ⚓

As a player and captain of the World Cup-winning Argentina side of 1978, Daniel Passarella provided the steel backbone that allowed the likes of Kempes, Luque and Ardiles to strut their stuff. When he graduated to manager in 1994, he proved that he had lost none of his no-nonsense approach. Long-haired players and players with earrings were told in no uncertain terms that they did not have a future in the Argentine team. There were complaints – but when the players realised Passarella was serious even Gabriel Batistuta got his flowing locks cut, so as not to miss the World Cup.

⚓ CONTROVERSIAL TO THE LAST ⚓

Harald Schumacher, West Germany's goalkeeper and twice World Cup finalist, is perhaps best known for his assault on French defender Patrick Battiston in the 1982 semi-final. After losing his second World Cup final in 1986, he said he wanted to come back in 1990 and win the cup at his third attempt. But in 1987 he wrote a book and claimed 90 per cent of the players in the German Bundesliga did drugs! He was never picked for the German squad again after that. He went to Turkey and played league soccer there instead.

⚓ GONE IN 60 SECONDS ⚓

José Batista of Uruguay was sent off after just 56 seconds against Scotland in 1986. That is the fastest dismissal in World Cup history. His foul on Gordon Strachan gave French referee Joël Quiniou no choice. Uruguay kept the score at 0–0, however, and progressed to the next round at the expense of Scotland.

⚓ SUPER MARIO ⚓

Manager Mario Zagallo took Brazil to their 1970 triumph, thus becoming the first man to play in and then manage a World Cup-winning team. He was a member of the Brazilian sides which won the trophy in 1958 and 1962.

⚓ A BAFFLING DECISION BACKFIRES ⚓

One of the most controversial managerial decisions was made by Ademar Pimenta, coach of Brazil in 1938. Leonidas, one of the stars of that tournament, had scored six goals in two rounds, but was left out of the team for the semi-final against defending champions Italy because the manager wanted to save him for the final. Brazil lost the game, but won third place – with Leonidas back in the team scoring twice!

⚓ PENALTY KINGS ⚓

Penalty shoot-outs have played a vital part in recent World Cups. West Germany and Argentina have the best records, winning all three shoot-outs they have participated in. Italy on the other hand, have taken part in four and won just one – against France in the 2006 World Cup final.

⚓ FLAG OF CONVENIENCE ⚓

Five players who each have appeared for two nations in World Cups: José Altafini (then known as Mazzola) for Brazil in 1958 and Italy in 1962; Luis Monti for Argentina in 1930 and Italy in 1934; Ferenc Puskas for Hungary in 1954 and Spain 1962; José Santamaria for Uruguay in 1954 and Spain in 1962; and Robert Prosinecki for Yugoslavia in 1990 and Croatia in 1998. The rules have now changed, and no player can play for more than one country.

⚓ SINGLE WINNER ⚓

No final match had produced fewer than three goals until 1990 when West Germany beat Argentina by 1–0. The winning goal was scored from the penalty spot by Andreas Brehme.

⚓ UNBEATEN ZENGA ⚓

Italian goalkeeper Walter Zenga holds the record of longest unbeaten run in World Cup history. He played 517 minutes (almost six games) without letting in a goal in the 1990 tournament. Claudio Caniggia of Argentina ended his run in the semi-final, which Italy eventually lost on penalties.

⚓ CRUYFF'S TURN ⚓

The 1974 World Cup match between Sweden and Holland ended in a stale 0–0 draw, but was enlivened by a moment of magic by Dutch skipper Johan Cruyff, who bamboozled a Swedish defender with a drag-back manoeuvre which became known simply as the 'Cruyff Turn':

1 Cruyff, on the left wing, shapes to cross the ball.

2 He stops abruptly and lifts his leg at a 45-degree angle.

3 He drags the ball back behind his standing leg with the inside of his foot.

4 Now he spins round so his shoulders and hips are in line with the ball.

5 Defender beaten, Cruyff continues on his way.

3

1

4

2

5

⚓ X FINALLY RATED ⚓

When Daniel Xuereb of France came on as a substitute for Bruno Bellone in the semi-final against West Germany in 1986, it was a red-letter day for statistics nuts. The X meant that every letter in the alphabet had been used in players' surnames since the start of the championships in 1930.

⚓ GET THAT GOALKEEPER OFF! ⚓

Muampa Kazadi was the first goalkeeper to be replaced for any other reason than injury in World Cup history, when Zaïre were 0–3 down versus Yugoslavia after just 22 minutes in 1974. The only other time a goalkeeper has been replaced for any other reason than injury was in the third-place play-off in USA 1994, when Bulgarian keeper Mihailov was substituted at half-time with Sweden leading 4–0. Nikolov came in for him and kept a clean sheet in the second half.

⚓ GOAL-CRAZY FRANCE ⚓

In 1958, the French team won the third-place play-off 6–3 against West Germany – and in doing so took their goal tally for the tournament to an extraordinary 23 in just six games. Supreme marksman was Juste Fontaine, who bagged thirteen including four in the last match. It was a remarkable turn-around for the French who the previous November had been crushed 4–0 by England.

⚓ FERRINI FAILS TO WALK ⚓

Sent off by English referee Ken Aston just four minutes into his team's match with hosts Chile in 1962, Italian inside-forward Giorgio Ferrini refused to leave the pitch. Eventually, ten minutes later, the Italian was escorted to the changing rooms by two hefty armed policemen. It was not long before he was joined for an early bath by team-mate Mario David as the match known as the Battle of Santiago lurched into violent anarchy. With just nine of their men remaining on the pitch, Italy managed to hang on for 73 minutes before Chile opened the scoring, going on to win the match 2–0.

⚓ A TROPHY FIT FOR CHAMPIONS ⚓

The Jules Rimet Trophy was the original prize for winning the World Cup. Originally called simply the World Cup or *Coupe du Monde*, it was renamed in 1946 to honour the FIFA President Jules Rimet who in 1929 passed a vote to initiate the competition. It was designed by Abel Lafleur, standing 35 cm high and weighing 3.8 kg and made of gold-plated sterling silver. It was in the shape of a cup, incorporating a statuette of Nike, the ancient Greek goddess of victory.

The Jules Rimet Trophy

⚓ BRAZIL ⚓

Brazil's 3–1 defeat by Hungary at Goodison Park, home of Everton, during the 1966 World Cup finals in England was their first in the tournament since 1954 – when they were beaten 4–2 by Hungary.

⚓ ANIMALS? ⚓

England manager Alf Ramsey was so infuriated by what he perceived as foul play by Argentina in England's quarter-final match in the 1966 World Cup, he not only forbade his side to swap jerseys with the South Americans, but labelled them 'animals'. But were they? Argentina were indeed reduced to ten men after their captain Rattin was sent off – but his offence was more dissent than foul play. And in a letter to *The Times* a few days later, Lord Lovat of the Guards Club pointed out that in fact Argentina had only committed nineteen fouls in the game, compared with 33 by England.

⚓ ALF'S ADVICE ⚓

'You've won it once – now do it again.'
– England boss Alf Ramsey exhorts his troops before extra-time in the 1966 World Cup final

⚓ 1970 INNOVATIONS ⚓

The 1970 World Cup in Mexico saw two innovations that have become standard practice in football matches ever since. First, substitutes were allowed for the first time. Second, yellow and red cards were introduced.

⚓ FOOTBALL IS NOT A GAME OF LIFE AND DEATH – OR IS IT? ⚓

In order to qualify for the 1970 finals in Brazil, Honduras and El Salvador were drawn together in the same group. The rivalry between the two sides was such that the result was very nearly all-out war. The mayhem erupted as follows:

Prior to their match in Honduras, the El Salvador team were kept awake all night in their hotel by gangs of home supporters.

Honduras won the match 1–0 through a last-minute goal. Back in El Salvador, eighteen-year-old Amelia Bolianos was so distraught, she seized her father's pistol and shot herself through the heart. Her funeral was shown live on TV, ensuring that the second meeting between the two sides was conducted in an atmosphere of mounting hysteria.

On the eve of the second leg, El Salvador fans broke

into the Honduras hotel and pelted the players with rotten eggs and dead rats. The home team won 3–0 and Honduras required an armed convoy to get them back to the airport. Two of their fans were killed after the game, and many others kicked and beaten as they attempted to flee back across the border.

Incredibly the group finished with both El Salvador and Honduras forced to play a sudden-death play-off. Four days beforehand, diplomatic relations between the two nations were severed – but this was nothing compared with the three days of fighting that ensued after El Salvador had succeeded in winning the tie 3–2 in extra-time. When it was over, more than 3,000 people were dead.

⚓ WORLD CUP RECORDS ⚓

Oldest player: Cameroon's Roger Milla, who was 42 years and 39 days old when he played against Russia in 1994.

Youngest player: Norman Whiteside of Northern Ireland, who was just 17 years and 41 days old when he played against Yugoslavia in 1982.

Shortest World Cup career in terms of minutes on the field: Tunisia's Khemais Labidi, who played two minutes against Mexico in 1978, and Argentina's Marcelo Trobbiani, who played the last two minutes of his country's 3–2 final win over West Germany in 1986.

First World Cup substitute: Anatoli Puzach of the Soviet Union against Mexico in 1970. He replaced Shesterniev. Substitutes were never used until the 1970 World Cup.

First goalkeeper to be substituted: Steve Adamache of Romania against Brazil. He was injured and replaced by Necula Raducanu in 1970.

Fastest substitution: 1998, when Italy's Alessandro Nesta was replaced by Giuseppe Bergomi in the match against Austria after only four minutes.

The man who has refereed most matches: Joël Quiniou of France. He was in charge of eight matches between 1986 and 1994 with four of them coming in USA '94. Nicolaj Latychev (Russia, 1962), José Ramiz Wright (Brazil, 1990) and Jan Langenus (Belgium, 1930) have also refereed four times in one tournament – which is a record also.

Youngest referee: Francisco Mateuccia of Uruguay, aged 27 years and 62 days old when he officiated the match between Yugoslavia versus Bolivia in 1930.

Oldest referee: George Reader of England, aged 53 years and 236 days old when he reffed the Brazil–Uruguay World Cup-deciding match in 1950.

Youngest coach: Juan Jose Tramutola of Argentina, aged 27 years and 267 days old when his country opened their campaign against France in 1930.

Oldest coach: Gaston Barreau of France, aged 70 years and 194 days old when his country played Mexico in 1954. Cesare Maldini was 34 days younger when he coached Paraguay in 2002.

⚐ EDUCATION COMES FIRST ⚐

In the 1930 World Cup finals group stage, Argentina faced bitter South American rivals Mexico without their captain, Ferreyra, after he decided to return home to sit his university exams. It didn't make much difference – his side ran out 6–3 winners, with centre-forward Stabile becoming the first man to bag a World Cup hat-trick.

⚐ NO CROWD TROUBLE ⚐

When Romania met Peru in a group stage match in the 1930 finals, a crowd of just 300 people turned out to watch. Unfortunately, the match was played on Bastille Day, a public holiday in Uruguay, and most people in Montevideo had better things to do with their time than watch two foreign teams play football. By contrast when Uruguay played in the same stadium just four days later, nearly 100,000 fans filled the terraces.

⚐ NO COACH ⚐

Uruguay, hosts and winners of the 1930 World Cup finals, played all their matches without a coach. The players decided on the line-ups and the tactics between themselves over a convivial supper the night before a match.

⚓ SHOT PUTTERS ⚓

In 1930, the USA team was nicknamed 'The Shot Putters' by the French squad because of their muscular build. The side was mostly made up of ex-pat Brits who had conveniently been granted Green Card work permits by the US government in time for the finals in Uruguay.

⚓ OUT FOR THE COUNT ⚓

As touchline protests go, one of most futile was staged by the trainer of the USA side during their group match against Argentina in 1930. Incensed at a refereeing decision, he threw down his medical box in a fit of pique. Unfortunately this succeeded only in smashing a bottle of chloroform, which knocked him out and resulted in him being carried from the pitch. Out for the count, he missed his side being trounced 6–1.

⚓ BALLS! ⚓

The rivalry between Uruguay and Argentina was such that in the 1930 final, each half was played with a different ball manufactured in each country. Uruguay's 4–2 victory prompted riots in Buenos Aires, during which the Uruguayan embassy was stoned, and led to diplomatic relations between the two countries being suspended.

⚓ URUGUAY ABSENT ⚓

Still miffed at the general European apathy that meant only France, Yugoslavia, Romania and Belgium bothered to enter the 1930 finals, Uruguay refused to enter the 1934 competition held in Italy. They remain the only reigning World Cup champions who have failed to defend their title.

⚓ ESCAPE ROUTE ⚓

Belgian referee John Langenus was so concerned about the repercussions of officiating the 1930 final between Uruguay and Argentina, he not only demanded police protection in the stadium but a guaranteed escape route to the ship on which he and the rest of the Belgian party were staying.

⚐ BROTHERS IN ARMS ⚐

The Evaristo brothers of Argentina were the first to play together in a World Cup final when they turned out against Uruguay in 1930.

⚐ VISIT OF THE DUCE ⚐

Italian dictator Benito Mussolini was in no doubt that his presence would inspire his country in their opening game of the 1934 World Cup in Rome. Indeed, a newspaper editorial on the morning of the match crowed that Il Duce would be 'bestowing the privilege of his presence, which would galvanise the two teams more than any other coefficient'. It certainly galvanised the Italians, who crushed the USA 7–1.

⚐ CHOKED ⚐

Elmer Schroeder, manager of the 1934 USA team, died in 1953 – strangled with the cord of his own window blind.

⚐ POLE APART ⚐

Five years before Germany invaded Poland, their 1934 World Cup football team was captained by Fritz Szepan – a Pole.

⚐ FATHERS AND SONS ⚐

When Patrice Rio appeared for France in the 1978 World Cup finals he was following in the footsteps of his father, Roger, who played for France in the 1934 tournament. Similarly Jose Vantrola, who played for Mexico in 1970, was the son of Martin Vantrola, who starred in the Spanish midfield in 1934. Miguel Alonso played for Spain in Argentina in 1978 and when they hosted the 1982 World Cup finals. His son Xabi was in the Spanish squad which competed in the 2002 World Cup finals in Japan/South Korea.

⚓ POINTLESS ⚓

'It is of no purpose and it should not exist.'
– French manager Michel Hidalgo dismisses the third-place play-off in 1982

⚓ HERE COME CUBA ⚓

Cuba played Mexico three times during qualifying for the 1938 World Cup and lost every time. Yet they still made it to the finals in France – as a replacement for Mexico, who dropped out at the last minute.

⚓ DUTCH COURAGE ⚓

As World Cup outsiders go, the Dutch East Indies side which made it to the 1938 finals were possibly the most mismatched. Lining up for their first and last World Cup fixture against the mighty Hungarians, nine of their side were earning their first caps and eight of them were students. Their captain, Achmad Nawir, was a doctor whose short-sightedness meant he had to wear spectacles on the pitch. Unsurprisingly, they were hammered 6–0.

⚓ ALL CHANGE FOR ITALY ⚓

When Italy played France at the Colombes Stadium in Paris in 1938, a good proportion of the 58,000 crowd consisted of anti-Fascist Italians who had fled their homeland in order to escape the regime of dictator Benito Mussolini. Yet the hail of abuse which greeted their every touch seemed to inspire the Italians, who weathered tremendous French pressure to finish the first half level at 1–1. Realising that his side clearly played better in the face of adversity, Italian manager Vittorio Pozzo sent his team out for the second half wearing a change strip of all black – the preferred colour of the Fascist movement. His ploy worked like a charm as, despite the fury of the crowd, Italy ran out 3–1 winners.

⚓ GOALLESS RECORD ⚓

The 1958 clash between England and Brazil was the 105th World Cup match and, remarkably, the very first to end goalless.

⚓ 1966 AND ALL THAT – WHAT IF? ⚓

- John Connelly, Terry Paine and Ian Callaghan had played brilliantly in the group matches and kept their place in the starting eleven?
- Jimmy Greaves hadn't gashed his leg against France and therefore wasn't replaced by Geoff Hurst?
- Nobby Stiles had been sent off for a second bookable offence against France?
- Gordon Banks had been dropped for his erratic performance against Portugal in the semi-final and replaced by Ron Springett?
- Jack Charlton had been sent off for deliberate handball, giving away a penalty against Portugal? Then the England team in the final might have looked like this:

England v West Germany (1966 World Cup Final): Ron Springett; George Cohen, Bobby Moore (c), Norman Hunter, Ray Wilson; John Connelly, Terry Paine, Ian Callaghan, Bobby Charlton; Jimmy Greaves, Roger Hunt

⚓ MANLY PURSUITS ⚓

'He [Nobby Stiles] jumped on my back. It looked like copulation. I don't know what he was doing but I didn't enjoy it very much.'
– England World Cup winner George Cohen recalls Nobby Stiles's ecstatic celebration at the final whistle

⚓ FIREWORKS ⚓

The Maracana stadium in Rio was built especially for the 1950 World Cup – although it was far from being finished in time for the opening match between hosts Brazil and Mexico. Indeed much of the concrete was still drying when a pre-match 21-gun salute erupted on the pitch. Watching from the stands, English referee Arthur Ellis recalled how 'we were peppered with a shower of concrete, fortunately none of it in huge blocks!'

⚓ CAN I HAVE A WORD? ⚓

No sooner had Brazilian striker Ademir given his side the lead in their first match of the 1950 World Cup against Mexico than he was swamped by fifteen radio commentators and more than twenty newspaper reporters who had run onto the pitch in search of a quote.

⚑ LATE KICK-OFF ⚑

The 1950 tie between Yugoslavia and Switzerland in Belo Horizonte, Brazil, kicked off twenty minutes late while corner flags were found and a line of chairs, reserved for dignitaries, was moved from right next to one of the touchlines. Consequently, the match became the first to be completed under floodlights. The Yugoslavs won 3–0, with two of the goals being scored in the gloom of the last ten minutes.

⚑ WISE BEFORE THE EVENT ⚑

Prior to their match against Switzerland in 1950, Brazilian coach Flavio Costa arrogantly dismissed his European opponents as 'contenders without importance'. Fittingly, Costa required a police escort from the stadium to protect him from irate Brazil fans after his side could only manage a 2–2 draw.

⚑ SOLE REPORTER ⚑

The USA's 1–0 win over England in 1950 sent shockwaves around the footballing world – except in the States. Indeed there was only one American reporter in the ground to see the historic victory: Dent McSkimming of the St Louis Post Despatch, who was only present because he happened to be on holiday in Brazil at the time.

⚑ COLONIAL COINCIDENCE ⚑

On the same day as England were beaten by the USA in the 1950 World Cup, England's cricketers lost to the West Indies at home for the first time.

⚑ A REAL MOUTHFUL ⚑

TV coverage of the World Cup didn't begin in earnest until the 1962 finals in Chile. Which is just as well for football commentators around the world, because Turkey's Lefter Kucukandonyadis – the man with the longest surname in the history of the tournament – had retired after the 1954 tournament.

⚓ YOU'VE GOT TO START SOMEWHERE ⚓

The very first World Cup qualifier was played on 11 June 1933. Sweden beat Estonia 6–2.

⚓ LONG HAUL FOR THE 'REGGAE BOYZ' ⚓

If anyone deserved a place in the 1998 World Cup it was the self-styled 'Reggae Boyz' of Jamaica. After all, in order to reach France they had been forced to play an extraordinary twenty qualifying matches. After all that, they found themselves drawn in a group which included Argentina and Croatia who duly thrashed them 5–0 and 3–1 respectively. However, in their last group match against Japan the Reggae Boyz turned on the style and recorded a fine 2–1 win thanks to two goals from Theodore Whitmore. And as far as they were concerned, the result made the long haul worthwhile. 'Did the road really have to end that quick?' said captain Leroy Simpson after the match. 'I'm really ecstatic at the moment. I'm over the moon that we can actually leave the tournament on a high.'

⚓ LEND US A RUPEE? ⚓

Sri Lanka were forced to pull out of the 1978 World Cup qualification process because they couldn't afford FIFA's entrance fee.

⚓ LOWEST ATTENDANCE ⚓

It wasn't quite one man and his dog, but when Turkmenistan played Chinese Taipei in a qualifying game at Amman on 7 May 2001, the crowd was just twenty people. Those who could be bothered to attend saw Turkmenistan win by a single goal to nil.

⚓ AMATEUR EXCEPT FOR ALFREDO ⚓

In 1930 Argentina reached the World Cup final. But due to a row between various factions of the Argentine FA in the intervening four years, the 1934 squad was made up almost entirely of amateur players. Only skipper Alfredo Devincenzi had been capped before.

⚓ 'STURMTANK' ⚓

Robust Hungarian striker Geza Toldi was nicknamed 'Sturmtank' (Storm Tank) because of his frightening physique. In his first game of the 1934 World Cup finals he scored a goal by simply barging the Egyptian goalkeeper into the back of the net – a tactic which was regarded as perfectly acceptable at the time.

⚓ ARGENTINA ABSENT ⚓

Following their success in reaching the 1930 final, several of Argentina's top players were promptly poached by leading Italian clubs to the extent that one of them, Monti, actually qualified for residence and appeared for the *Azzurri* in the 1934 finals in Italy. To prevent further defections, the Argentine football authorities banned their star players from travelling to Italy – with the inevitable result that they were knocked out by Sweden in the first round.

⚓ ANNEXE ⚓

On 12 March 1938, Adolf Hitler invaded Austria. Not surprisingly, the Austrian team was withdrawn from that year's World Cup finals in France. However, five of their leading players (Hahnemann, Raftl, Schmaus, Skoumal, Neumer and Stroh) did play in the tournament – for Germany, who claimed that since Austria had been annexed, the men qualified for the Fatherland. To Hitler's fury, such rule-bending was to no avail. Germany were eliminated in the first round by Switzerland.

⚓ BRAZIL ARROGANCE ⚓

In 1938 Brazil clearly believed their name was on the Jules Rimet trophy. Having drawn with Czechoslovakia in a bloody first-round match, the South Americans duly dispatched most of their squad to Marseille in advance of the replay, anticipating a semi-final tie against Italy. The gamble paid off, and they won 2–1. In the semi-final, the Brazilians were so confident of victory that they rested their star strikers Leonidas and Tim and fielded what amounted to a second-string side. This time, they ended up with egg on their face as the Italians ran out 2–1 winners and proceeded to win their second successive World Cup.

⚓ POZZO'S PRETEXT ⚓

Vittorio Pozzo is the only man to manage two World Cup-winning sides, leading Italy to the trophy in 1934 and 1938. A keen student of the game, who compiled lengthy dossiers on his opponents, Pozzo was also a keen rule-bender who selected Argentinian-born players on the flimsy pretext that they were eligible for Italian national service. 'If they can die for Italy, they can play for Italy!' was one of his maxims.

⚓ INDIA BAREFOOT ⚓

India withdrew from the 1950 World Cup finals in Brazil after FIFA officials told them they could not play barefoot.

⚓ SCOTLAND FEEL THE HEAT ⚓

Perhaps believing that Switzerland was snowbound all year round, the Scotland team arrived at the 1954 World Cup finals with kit that included thick woolly jerseys with long sleeves. Unfortunately, temperatures in Basle topped 100 degrees during their group matches. 'You'd have thought we were going on an expedition to the Antarctic,' said wing-half Tommy Docherty. It was no surprise, therefore, that the Scots were soon on their way home after losing 1–0 to Austria and being crushed 7–0 by Uruguay.

⚓ SWISS CAPTAIN ⚓

Captain of the 1954 Swiss team was Roger Bocquet, a normally highly competent defender. But, having swept to a 3–0 lead in a group match against Austria, the Swiss inexplicably collapsed to lose 5–4. Prime culprit was Bocquet himself, who gifted a couple of goals and to many observers appeared to be playing as if in a trance. It was only later that it was revealed Bocquet was suffering from a brain tumour and had played against medical advice.

⚓ SNOW ON MEXICO ⚓

Despite the advantage of playing against European opposition in South America, Mexico were thrashed by France 4–1 in the first ever World Cup match in Montevideo, Uruguay in 1930. Oddly, the Mexicans complained about the weather – as the night before it had snowed.

⚓ YOUNG STARTER ⚓

Juan Jose Tramutola was, at 27 years and 267 days, the youngest ever World Cup coach when he masterminded Argentina's assault on the 1930 tournament in Uruguay.

⚓ WHO'S THE BOLIVIAN IN THE BLACK? ⚓

Such was the convivial nature of the first World Cup in 1930, when Argentina played Mexico the referee was also the manager of Bolivia while the linesman was the Romanian boss.

⚓ VIVA BOLIVIA ⚓

Determined to make a good impression, Bolivia took to the pitch for their 1930 clash against Yugoslavia with each player sporting a letter of the alphabet on the front of his white shirt, forming the words 'VIVA URUGUAY'. Yugoslavia thrashed them 4–0.

⚓ BERET SPORTING ATTIRE ⚓

When Bolivia played Brazil in 1930, three players from each side were sporting berets.

⚓ MY BROTHER ⚓

Star of the 1930 Uruguay side, Pedro Gestido had another claim to fame. His brother Oscar was the country's president.

⚓ AMERICAN CLUBS ⚓

In order to make up a squad for the 1930 World Cup, selectors from the USA were forced to scour obscure ex-pat clubs for players. Hence while other teams boasted players from the likes of Santos, River Plate and Milan, the Americans came from the likes of Wiebolt Wonderbolts, Detroit Holley Carburettor, Curry Silver Tops and Providence Clamdiggers.

⚓ THE BATTLE OF BERNE ⚓

It took only three minutes for the 1954 match between Hungary and Brazil to disintegrate into what one commentator has described as 'psychopathic violence, disorder and anarchy'. That was how long it took Hungary's Hidegkuti to score the opening goal, prompting outrageous scenes in which he was mobbed by the Brazilians and had his shorts ripped off. The rest of the game was punctuated by a series of increasingly horrific fouls and outrageous play-acting. English referee Arthur Ellis did his best to control the mayhem, but meltdown occurred with fifteen minutes remaining and Hungary leading 3–2. Brazil's Santos and Hungary's Bozsik (an upstanding member of the Hungarian parliament) were sent off for fighting. The Brazilian trainer ran on to protest and was escorted off the pitch by Swiss police. A few minutes later, with Hungary now 4–2 ahead, Brazil's Humberto launched a flying kick at Lorant and was ordered off by Mr Ellis. His departure was delayed by a bizarre interlude in which the player sank to his knees and begged the referee to be allowed to stay on the pitch. But if the game itself was a disgrace, worse was to follow after the final whistle. As the Hungarians celebrated their victory in the changing room, bottles were thrown at them. Seconds later the lightbulb was smashed and suddenly the Hungarians found themselves being set upon by the Brazilians. In the all-out scrap that followed, Hoth was knocked unconscious and Sebes had his cheek cut open. Had they not already been on their way home, the Brazilians would surely have been kicked out of the tournament they had so comprehensively tarnished.

⚓ FIRST DEFEAT ⚓

Uruguay's 4–2 defeat to Hungary in the semi-final of the 1954 tournament was their first ever World Cup loss.

⚓ PICKLES RIP ⚓

In 1966 Pickles the dog found the Jules Rimet trophy and saved the English FA from extreme embarrassment. Unfortunately there wasn't such a happy ending for Pickles himself. In 1971, while chasing a cat up a tree, the dog fell from the lower branches and was hanged by his own lead.

⚓ GREAT GAMES: ITALY 3–2 BRAZIL, 1982 ⚓

Paolo Rossi had been brought in from his match-fixing exile to provide Italy with goals – but up until this second-round match in Barcelona he had barely touched the ball. What a time he picked to wake up, against a Brazil side which had destroyed all before them with a breathtaking display of skill and goalscoring, and which only required a draw to proceed to the semi-finals. Rossi struck after just five minutes with a typical poacher's finish from close range. Brazil hit back almost immediately through the elegant Socrates, but then Cerezo gifted Rossi a second with a stray back-pass. With 68 minutes gone, Falcao blasted home a characteristically sublime long-range shot which surely meant the Brazilians were through. But this was Rossi's day: with sixteen minutes remaining, the little striker turned in the penalty area to shoot past Waldir Perez. Even then there was still time for high drama as Oscar looked certain to score with a header only for veteran Dino Zoff to pull off one of the saves of his career and send Italy into the semis.

⚓ REST HOME ⚓

West Germany's 3–2 victory over the mighty Hungary side of Hidegkuti, Kocsis and Puskas in the final of the 1954 World Cup was one of the greatest upsets in the history of the competition. But it was also wreathed in controversy. Just days after the final, several of the Germans checked into rest homes. Although they claimed it was to recover from the rigours of the tournament, it was rumoured that the real reason was to recover from the performance-enhancing drugs which had helped them to their first World Cup triumph.

⚓ WALES TAKE THE LONG ROAD ⚓

Wales have only qualified for the World Cup once, in 1958. Amazingly, their route to the finals in Sweden was courtesy of the Asia/Africa qualifying section. Egypt and Sudan were excluded due to the inflamed Middle East situation, while Indonesia's ongoing political struggles meant they had more pressing matters than qualifying for the World Cup. The fourth member of the group, Israel, was left with no opponent – but tournament regulations insisted that no team other than the host and the holder could proceed to the finals without first playing a qualifying match. As a result, the runners-up in eight other groups drew lots for a place in a special play-off. Wales were the lucky team and, by defeating Israel twice, proceeded to the finals.

⚓ HOME COUNTRIES ⚓

The 1958 finals in Sweden are the only time all four Home Union countries have qualified for the latter stages.

⚓ THE MIGHTY IRISH ⚓

Northern Ireland rarely grace World Cup finals, but when they do they always succeed in defying all expectations. In 1958 the men in green had already signalled their intent by beating Italy 2–1 in Belfast to reach the finals, and once in Sweden the team continued to confound the nay-sayers by pulling off a string of sensational results. In their first game they beat Czechoslovakia 1–0. The next match saw them play the powerful West Germany, holders of the cup. Widely expected to be thrashed, an Irish side including Danny Blanchflower, Derek Dougan and Peter McParland gave the Germans the fright of their lives. Only a Uwe Seeler thunderbolt in the dying minutes secured a 2–2 draw. A comprehensive defeat by Argentina in their next match left the Irish needing to win a play-off against Czechoslovakia. Miraculously, with just nine fit players on the field, Blanchflower's men managed to win in extra-time. Despite losing the quarter-final 4–0 to France, the Northern Ireland players returned home as heroes.

⚓ DISASTER FOR SCOTLAND! ⚓

In qualifying for World Cup finals, Scotland invariably show a passion and unity of purpose which, for some inexplicable reason, seems to disintegrate the minute their plane lands. Here is their World Cup tale of woe so far: it is not for the fainthearted.

1950: The Scots qualify for Brazil by finishing runners-up to England in a qualifying group based on the Home International championship. However the Scottish FA petulantly carry out their threat to withdraw from the tournament if they are not British champions.

1954: Having reached Switzerland in fine style, the Scots swiftly self-destruct. They lose to Austria then, after a row with the Scottish FA, manager Andy Beattie quits on the eve of the pool game against Uruguay. The team are duly hammered 7–0, having been sent onto the park in 100 degree heat with woollen, long-sleeved shirts.

1958: The Scottish FA appoint Matt Busby as manager for the tournament in Brazil. Just weeks later, Busby is seriously injured in the Munich air crash and is replaced by Dawson Walker. Despite gaining their first World Cup goal and point in a 1–1 draw with Yugoslavia, the Scots lose three influential players to injury and lose 3–2 to Paraguay. A draw against France would give them a chance of reaching the quarter-finals, but with minutes to go and trailing 2–1, the Scots miss a penalty.

1974: Having missed out on three World Cup finals, the Scots are understandably overjoyed to qualify for West Germany as Britain's sole representatives. So much so that leading players Billy Bremner and Willie Johnston are threatened with expulsion by the Scottish FA after missing a curfew during a warm-up tour in Norway. For a while, things go well on the pitch. A 2–0 win over lowly Zaire is followed by an encouraging goalless draw against the world champions Brazil. A draw will suffice against Yugoslavia, as long as Brazil score less than three clear goals against Zaire. Scotland play abysmally and can only salvage a draw through a last minute goal by Joe Jordan. Inevitably, Brazil win 3–0. Despite remaining the only unbeaten team in the entire tournament, Scotland are on their way home.

1978: The Tartan Army, Britain's sole representatives once again, fly into Argentina on a wave of frenzied expectation, chiefly orchestrated by their manager Ally MacLeod and by the bookies who have laid odds of 8–1 that they will win the competition. There is therefore a huge sense of anticlimax in watching the team utterly humiliated by Peru, who beat them 3–1, and Iran, who contrive a 1–1 draw. Needing to beat Holland by three clear goals to qualify for the next stage, the Scots pull out their best performance of the tournament – but win 3–2. Once again they are on the early flight home, although they are beaten to it by winger Willie Johnston who has already been sent home in disgrace after failing a drugs test.

1982: Leading 3–0 in their first group match against lowly New Zealand things at last appear to be going to plan for Scotland. But then New Zealand score twice and suddenly it is panic stations. Although two late Scottish goals calm the nerves slightly, it does not bode well for the Tartan Army – especially as their next opponents are Brazil. And so it proves. Despite scoring one of the goals of the tournament through David Narey, the Scots are skewered by the skills of Zico, Falcao, Socrates and Junior, and are fortunate to escape with a 4–1 hiding. Needing to beat the USSR to progress there is a sad inevitability about the gallant but futile, 2–2 draw which eliminates them on goal difference.

⚊ WORLD CUP FACTS, UP TO AND INCLUDING 2010 FINALS ⚊

MOST PARTICIPATIONS (TEAM)

Brazil 19
Germany 17
Italy 17
Argentina 15
Mexico 14

MOST APPEARANCES BY A PLAYER

Lothar Matthaus (West Germany/Germany):
25, 1982–98
Paolo Maldini (Italy): 23, 1990–2002
Uwe Seeler (West Germany): 21, 1958–1970
Wladislaw Zmuda (Poland): 21, 1970–1986
Diego Maradona (Argentina): 21, 1982–1994

MOST GOALS IN ONE COMPETITION

Hungary: 27, 1954
West Germany: 25, 1954
France: 23, 1958
Brazil: 22, 1950
Brazil: 19, 1970

MOST COMPETITIONS BY A PLAYER

Antonio Carbajal (Mexico): 5, 1950–66
Lothar Matthaus
(West Germany/Germany): 5, 1982–98

MOST HAT-TRICKS

2, Sándor Kocsis (Hungary, 1954), Just
Fontaine (France, 1958), Gerd Müller (West
Germany, 1970), and Gabriel Batistuta
(Argentina, 1994 and 1998).

YOUNGEST GOALSCORER

17 years and 239 days, Pelé
(Brazil, vs Wales, 1958).

OLDEST GOALSCORER

42 years and 39 days, Roger Milla
(Cameroon, vs Russia, 1994).

BIGGEST WINS

Hungary 10–1 ....El Salvador, 1982
Hungary 9–0 ....South Korea, 1954
Yugoslavia 9–0 ....Zaire, 1974
Sweden 8–0 ....Cuba, 1938
Uruguay 8–0 ....Bolivia, 1950
Germany 8–0 ....Saudi Arabia, 2002

⚓ WORLD CUP STOLEN ⚓

It was perhaps the proudest moment in the history of the English Football Association – but it was to turn into a huge embarrassment.

Having been awarded the 1966 World Cup finals, the FA were obviously keen to promote the event at every opportunity. In March that year, the committee got hold of the £30,000 solid gold Jules Rimet trophy and put it on display at the 'Sport with Stamps' exhibition at Central Hall in Westminster, London.

During a church service taking place in another part of the building, the unthinkable happened and, despite the presence of two guards, the trophy was stolen. In what was thought to be an opportunistic theft, the thieves left stamps worth £3 million.

According to police, a 'suspicious-looking man' was seen in the building at the time of the theft. He was described as being in his early thirties, of average height with thin lips, greased black hair and a possible scar on his face.

Vice-chairman of the Football Association Council Jack Stewart was reluctant to accept blame for the trophy's disappearance. But he admitted: 'We are responsible for it in the end because we are the organizing association.'

This was little comfort to Brazil, who had been holders of the Cup for the previous eight years, after winning both the 1958 and 1962 competitions. After several days, it seemed that the famous trophy was gone for ever. Then, on 27 March, a week after the theft, David Corbett, a Thames lighterman, saw his mongrel dog Pickles scratching at something wrapped in newspaper in a garden near his South London home. To his astonishment, inside was the Jules Rimet trophy. A little over two months later, Corbett was watching as the trophy was lifted by victorious England skipper Bobby Moore.

⚓ THE MATTHEWS FINALS ⚓

England's Stanley Matthews was not only the oldest
player at the 1950 World Cup finals, aged 35, but at the
1954 finals in Switzerland, where he appeared aged 39.

⚓ SWEDEN'S CRAZY RULE ⚓

Sweden pulled off one of the shocks of the 1950 World Cup when they
defeated Italy 3–2 in a group match in Sao Paulo. More remarkably, they
did so without three of their best players. The inside-forward trio of
Gren, Nordahl and Liedholm had been signed by AC Milan the previous
season, and the Swedish FA refused to pick players who played for
foreign clubs. This policy was quickly changed after the World Cup,
when almost the entire Swedish squad were signed by Italian clubs.

⚓ THE FINALS ⚓

1930

URUGUAY (1) 4
Dorado 12, Cea 57, Iriarte 68, Castro 89
ARGENTINA (2) 2
Peucelle 20, Stabile 37

Date: 30 July 1930
Venue: Centenario, Montevideo
Attendance: 93,000
Referee: John Langenus (BEL)

Uruguay took the lead through Dorado, but the goal was cancelled out eight
minutes later when winger Peucelle dodged two tackles to fire home from the
edge of the box. Argentina, playing with flair and skill compared with the
hosts' rugged style, then stunned the home crowd by taking the lead through
Stabile. In the second half, however, Uruguay's physical approach and the
effect of the huge partisan crowd began to tell. Cea levelled the scores after
57 minutes and then Argentina wilted under waves of Uruguayan pressure.
First Iriarte beat the keeper with a dipping long-range shot, then, in the dying
seconds Castro looped a header into the net to confirm the win.

URUGUAY: *Ballestro, Nasazzi (c), Mascheroni, Andrade, Fernandez,
Gestido, Dorado, Scarone, Castro, Cea, Iriarte*
ARGENTINA: *Botasso, Della Torre, Paternoster, J Evaristo, Monti,
Suarez, Peucelle, Varallo, Stabile, Ferreira (c), M Evaristo*

1934

ITALY (0) (1) 2
Orsi 81, Schiavo 95
CZECHOSLOVAKIA (0) (1) 1 (AET)
Puc 71

Date: 10 June 1934
Venue: Nazionale del PNF, Rome
Attendance: 50,000
Referee: Ivan Eklind (SWE)

A grim battle of attrition saw Italy and Czechoslovakia grind out a goalless first half. The second looked to be heading the same way until a moment of genius from Czech winger Puc transformed the match on 71 minutes. Receiving the ball way out, he sliced through the Italian defence and drew the keeper before smashing it home inside the near post. It was a remarkable goal because only minutes earlier Puc had been carried off dazed from a crunching tackle and had to be given a whiff of ammonia to unscramble his senses. Suddenly the Czechs were rampant, hitting the post and firing just over the bar. Then, with nine minutes remaining and totally against the run of play, Italy equalised. Orsi collected the ball on the edge of the box, dummied to shoot with his left foot then curled an unstoppable shot into the net with the outside of his right. The crowd – which included Mussolini – went wild; the game went into extra-time. Five minutes in, Guaita found Schiavo unmarked on the edge of the box and his low cross shot beat the Czech keeper and flew into the net. There was no way back for Czechoslovakia and Italy had secured their first World Cup.

ITALY: Combi (c), Monzeglio, Allemandi, Ferraris, Monti, Bertolini, Guaita, Meazza, Schiavo, Ferrari, Orsi
CZECHOSLOVAKIA: Planicka (c), Zenisek, Ctyroky, Kostalek, Cambal, Krcil, Junek, Svoboda, Sobotka, Nejedly, Puc

1938

ITALY (3) 4
Colaussi 6, 35, Piola 16, 82
HUNGARY (1) 2
Titkos 7, Sarosi 69

Date: 19 June 1938
Venue: Stade Colombes, Paris
Attendance: 45,124
Referee: Georges Capdeville (FRA)

A second successive World Cup for Italy, but achieved with considerably more ease than their first. The Italians were ahead after just six minutes, but despite equalising almost immediately the Hungarian defence spent the first half at sixes and sevens as Piola and Biavati cut them to ribbons. Piola restored the lead on sixteen minutes, having just hit the post, then was instrumental in creating Colaussi's second after 35 minutes. Shell-shocked, Hungary rallied in the second half and pulled a goal back through Sarosi – but with eight minutes remaining Piola sent Briavati away down the right-hand side and was on hand to hammer home the cross. Italian skipper Meazza received the trophy with a Fascist salute to the watching Mussolini, a last symbolic act as Europe teetered on the brink of war.

ITALY: Olivieri, Foni, Rava, Serantoni, Andreolo, Locatelli, Biavati, Meazza (c), Piola, Ferrari, Colaussi
HUNGARY: Szabo, Polgar, Biro, Szalay, Szucs, Lazar, Sas, Vincze, Sarosi (c), Zsengeller, Titkos

1950

URUGUAY (0) 2
Schiaffino 66, Ghiggia 79
BRAZIL (0) 1
Friaca 47

Date: 16 July 1950
Venue: Maracana, Rio de Janeiro
Attendance: 205,000
Referee: George Reader (ENG)

FIFA, in their wisdom, decided that the first World Cup after the war would not be decided by a final tie but by a final group, the winners of which would be crowned champions. So it was that on 9 July Brazil, Spain, Sweden and Uruguay began a tortuous series of round-robin matches that would finally climax nine days later. When Brazil demolished Sweden and Spain 7-1 and 6-1 respectively, they must have felt they had one hand on the trophy. In their final pool match they needed only a draw against Uruguay – who had drawn against Spain and scored a last-gasp winner against Sweden – to confirm their position as undisputed champions. Yet, in front of a staggering 205,000 in the Maracana Stadium – the biggest crowd ever to watch a football match – Brazil fluffed their lines. Despite more than 30 shots at goal they could score only once, through Friaca, two minutes into the second half. This was never going to be enough against a typically robust Uruguayan side. Inspired by the willowy Ghiggia, they began to carve huge holes in the Brazil back line and it was no surprise when Schiaffino glanced home the equaliser from a cross by Ghiggia. With the vast terraces screaming with anguish, Uruguay came again and, with eleven minutes remaining, Ghiggia's cross shot was misjudged by goalkeeper Barbosa and crossed the line for the decisive goal. It was a major upset, but Brazil had only themselves to blame. Their footballing philosophy was based on having the greatest attack in the world. Conceding a goal or two didn't matter as long as they were scoring six or seven at the other end. In 1950 they should have learned their lesson, yet this would not be the last time a Brazil side would lose a World Cup they should have won at a canter.

URUGUAY: Maspoli, M Gonzalez, Tejera. Gambetta. Varela (c), Rodgriguez, Andrade, Ghiggia, Perez, Miguez, Schiaffino, Moran
BRAZIL: Barbosa, Augusto (c), Juvenal, Bauer, Danilo, Bigode, Friaca, Zizinho, Ademir, Jair, Chico

1954

WEST GERMANY (2) 3
Morlock 10, Rahn 19, 85
HUNGARY (2) 2
Puskas 6, Czibor 8

Date: 4 July 1954
Venue: Wankdorf Stadium, Berne
Attendance: 62,472
Referee: Bill Ling (ENG)

A Hungary team which had laid waste to all before them for two years should have won the 1954 World Cup without breaking sweat, and up until the final they appeared to be doing just that. But the Magic Magyars were about to learn that the competition is no respecter of class or form, and Puskas, Hidegkuti and co. were put to the sword by a West German side that would provide a blueprint for efficiency and together-ness of purpose.

Having thrashed the Germans 8–3 in the group stage, at first it seemed like business as usual as Puskas and Czibor nonchalantly prodded Hungary two-nil in front after just eight minutes. But this time the Germans, fielding six players from Kaiserslauten, were having none of it. The Magyars suddenly found their intricate triangles and first-time passing being stifled by German pressure. Morlock pounced on a rare defensive error to score after ten minutes, and after twenty the Germans were level through Rahn. In the second half Hungary attacked as if their lives depended on it, but Germany remained resolute. With five minutes left Shafer crossed the ball and defender Lantos could only head the ball weakly into the path of the predatory Rahn, who smashed it home. It was the end of a 32-match unbeaten run and earned Hungary the unwanted title of 'best team never to win the World Cup'.

WEST GERMANY: Turek, Posipal, Kohlmeyer, Eckel, Liebrich, Mai, Rahn, Morlock, O Walter, F Walter (c), Shafer
HUNGARY: Grosics, Buzansky, Lantos, Bozsik, Lorant, Zakarias, Czibor, Kocsis, Hidegkuti, Puskas (c), Toth

1958

BRAZIL (2) 5
Vava 9, 32, Pelé 55, 90, Zagallo 68
SWEDEN (1) 2
Liedholm 4, Simonsson 79

Date: 29 June 1958
Venue: Rasunda Stadium, Stockholm
Attendance: 49,737
Referee: Maurice Guigue (FRA)

It was eight years since Brazil had flopped so ignominiously against Uruguay, and they were determined that this time they would put matters right. And, although they scored after just four minutes, Sweden were never in the hunt against a side brimming with talent such as Didi, Vava, Garrincha and Pelé. The old Brazilian adage of attack being the best form of defence proved irresistible as Garrincha and Vava combined twice to shred the Swedish defence and give the South Americans the lead after 32 minutes. Ten minutes after the interval it was all over: Pelé, just seventeen years old, took a cross from Nilton Santos on his chest, flipped the ball over Gustavsson with his thigh, and drilled the ball past Svensson as it came down. Zagallo hit a fourth on 68 minutes and although Simonsson clipped home a second for Sweden after 79 minutes it did nothing to stop the Brazilian juggernaut. In the dying seconds, Pelé effortlessly backheeled the ball to Zagallo before running into the box to meet the cross. His header looped over the helpless Svensson, leaving the goalkeeper wrapped around his own post. It was an image which summed up Brazil's superiority on a day when every component of their supercharged engine ran to its full potential.

BRAZIL: Gylmar, D Santos, N Santos, Zito, Bellini (c), Orlando, Garrincha, Didi, Vava, Pelé, Zagallo
SWEDEN: Svensson, Bergmark, Axbom, Borjesson, Gustavsson, Parling, Hamrin, Gren, Simonsson, Liedholm (c), Skoglund

1962

BRAZIL (1) 3
Amarildo 16, Zito 69, Vava 78
CZECHOSLOVAKIA (1) 1
Masopust 14

Date: 17 June 1962
Venue: Nacional Stadium, Santiago
Attendance: 68,679
Referee: Nikolai Latyshev (USSR)

Although never as emphatic as their win against Sweden in 1958, Brazil comfortably retained the World Cup against a limited Czech side who had held the champions to a goalless draw in the group stage but could not suppress them a second time. Brazil began the final in customary fashion, by conceding an early goal. But, as usual, they equalised in a matter of minutes through Amarildo. After that, it was one-way traffic; the only surprise being that it took the Brazilians until the 69th minute to score again, Zito heading home Amarildo's clever cross. Even without the injured Pelé, Brazil's firepower was far too strong for the Czechs, and ten minutes later the irrepressible Vava rounded it off with a simple tap-in after keeper Schrojf had dropped the ball. With their two consecutive World Cup wins, Brazil were taking the game to previously unexplored levels – and the best was yet to come.

BRAZIL: Gylmar, D Santos, N Santos, Zito, Mauro (c), Zozimo, Garrincha, Didi, Vava, Amarildo, Zagallo
CZECHOSLOVAKIA: Schroijf, Tichy, Novak (c), Pluskal, Popluhar, Masopust, Pospichal, Scherer, Kadraba, Kvasnak, Jelinek

1966

ENGLAND (1) (2) 4
Hurst 19, 100, 119, Peters 78
WEST GERMANY (1) (2) 2 (AET)
Haller 13, Weber 89

Date: 30 July 1966
Venue: Wembley Stadium, London
Attendance: 93,802
Referee: Gottfried Dienst (SWI)

Having underperformed in their previous World Cup tournaments England failed to set this one alight until the latter stages. Fortunately, they were keeping the best till last. In front of 93,000 fans at Wembley Alf Ramsey's men showed reserves of stamina, resolve and courage that were previously thought to be the sole preserves of their opponents West Germany.

Things couldn't have started worse for England. After thirteen minutes, Wilson made a hash of an innocuous-looking cross from Held. The ball fell to Haller who drilled it home from the edge of the penalty area. Six minutes later, England's West Ham connection combined for the first time. Using a move which had been perfected on the training ground at Upton Park, Bobby Moore clipped a quick free-kick into the box where his Hammers team-mate Geoff Hurst – a replacement for the injured arch-predator Jimmy Greaves – had drifted in unmarked to head the ball home.

For an hour the game was attritional. There were few chances, neither side willing to make the mistake that might cost them the match and the World Cup. Then, on 78 minutes, England won a corner. Alan Ball floated it in, Hurst's shot from the edge of the box was blocked, and Martin Peters was on hand to smash it into the net from just seven yards. It should have been all over then – but the Germans, marshalled by Schulz, Hottges and the youngster Beckenbauer, did not believe in surrender. With less than a minute remaining, Jack Charlton was harshly penalised and when Emmerich hammered the free-kick into the box the ball pinballed to the near post where Weber was lurking to put it into the back of the net.

It was extra-time for the first time since 1934, and it belonged to Geoff Hurst. Ten minutes in, the indefatigable Ball got the better of Emmerich on the right and crossed long from the corner flag. Hurst controlled the ball, swivelled and struck it with venom against the underside of the crossbar. Forty years on, debate still rages as to whether the ball crossed the line, but what matters is that Azerbaijani linesman Tofik Bakhramov thought it had. England were ahead again, and this time it was a sucker punch from which even the Germans could not recover. The game was won long before Hurst latched onto Bobby Moore's through ball and smashed it into the net from 20 yards.

England were World Champions at last, and they had won the trophy the hard way. Few would deny them their moment of glory.

ENGLAND: Banks, Cohen, Wilson, Stiles, J Charlton, Moore (c), Ball, Hurst, R Charlton, Hunt, Peters
WEST GERMANY: Tilkowski, Hottges, Schnellinger, Beckenbauer, Schulz, Weber, Held, Haller, Seeler (c), Overath, Emmerich

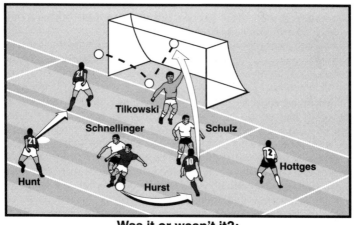

Was it or wasn't it?:
Geoff Hurst's controversial second goal

1970

BRAZIL (1) 4
Pelé 18, Gerson 66, Jairzinho 71, Carlos Alberto 86
ITALY (1) 1
Boninsegna 37

Date: 21 June 1970
Venue: Azteca Stadium, Mexico City
Attendance: 107,412
Referee: Rudi Glockner (East Germany)

In 1962 Brazil had been unstoppable. Now they were simply awesome. Fielding what many still believe to be the greatest team ever assembled for a World Cup finals, they annihilated a strong Italy with a verve and style which had not been seen before or since.

For once it was Brazil who got the early goal, and inevitably it was Pelé who scored it. Aged 29 and making his World Cup swansong, the 5ft 9in genius seemed to defy gravity as he leapt to meet Rivelino's cross in the 18th minute. A split-second later the ball was in the back of the net: it is doubtful whether goalkeeper Albertosi even saw it.
Yet despite their virtuosity, Brazil were still susceptible to defensive howlers – and on 37 minutes a lazy backheel by Clodoaldo allowed Boninsegna in for a goal which Italy scarcely deserved.

No matter: the equaliser simply made the destruction which followed in the second half all the more spectacular. Gerson and Jairzinho scored after Pelé had had a goal disallowed and Rivelino had hit the bar with a free kick. Then, with four minutes left, Clodoaldo held off several challenges in his own half before feeding Jairzinho on the left. The ball came to Pelé on the edge of the box and his leisurely but perfectly-paced square pass was met full-on by the skipper Carlos Alberto, whose right foot shot nearly ripped the netting out of the ground.

It was a stunning climax to a dazzling tournament for Brazil. They had now won the World Cup three times, but even though they would go on to win it on two further occasions nothing would compare to this.

BRAZIL: *Felix, Carlos Alberto (c), Everaldo, Clodoaldo, Brito, Piazza, Jairzinho, Gerson, Tostao, Pelé, Rivelino*
ITALY: *Albertosi, Burgnich, Facchetti (c), Bertini [Juliano 74], Rosato, Cera, Domenghini, Mazzola, Boninsegna [Rivera 84], De Sisti, Riva*

1974

WEST GERMANY (2) 2
Breitner pen 25, Muller 43
HOLLAND (1) 1
Neeskens pen 2

Date: 7 July 1974
Venue: Olympic Stadium, Munich
Attendance: 77,833
Referee: Jack Taylor (ENG)

World Cup finals had a tendency towards early goals, but none as early as the one which broke the deadlock in the 1974 final between hosts West Germany and Holland. Barely two minutes had gone when Dutch maestro Johan Cruyff's mazy run towards the German goal was ended when he was upended in the area by Uli Hoeness. English referee Jack Taylor pointed to the spot and Neeskens coolly sent Sepp Maier the wrong way. It was a sensational start and one which stunned the capacity crowd at Munich's impressive Olympic Stadium.

The goal should have been the springboard for the superb Dutch side, inspired by Cruyff, to go on to win their first World Cup – yet the side who had lit up the tournament with their magnificent brand of Total Football seemed uncertain how to proceed, whether to defend their lead or go all out to humiliate the hated Germans. In the end the chink of light they offered was exploited to the full by their pragmatic opponents.

With Vogts patrolling Cruyff, the Dutch seemed bereft of ideas, almost panic-stricken. The Germans came back strongly, and after 25 minutes Holzenbein went sprawling in the box under Jansen's challenge and Taylor once again pointed to the spot. Breitner hammered the ball home and suddenly it was the Germans who were in the ascendant.

Two minutes before the break, Bonhof left Ari Haan for dead and clipped the ball back across from the by-line to where the unmistakable figure of Gerd Muller was lurking. At first it seemed Muller had let the chance escape – but almost with his back to goal, the ace marksman swivelled and planted the ball past the static Jongbloed.

In the second half the Germans gave Holland an object lesson in how to defend a lead. Captain Beckenbauer, in his third World Cup, was outstanding, as was Vogts, in stemming the orange tide of pressure. Maier made a great save from Neeskens, but with Cruyff neutralised the threat was minimised.

After the pyrotechnics of 1970 it was not pretty – but it was mightily effective. The Germans had the honour of being the first team to lift the newly minted FIFA World Cup Trophy.

WEST GERMANY: Maier, Vogts, Breitner, Bonhof, Schwarzenbeck, Beckenbauer (c), Grabowski, Hoeness, Muller, Overath, Holzenbein
HOLLAND: Jongbloed, Suurbier, Krol, Jansen, Rijsbergen [de Jong 68], Haan, Rep, Neeskens, van Hanegen, Cruyff (c), Rensenbrink [R van der Kerkhof HT]

1978

ARGENTINA (1) (1) 3
Kempes 37, 104, Bertoni 115
HOLLAND (0) (1) 1 (AET)
Nanninga 82

Date: 25 June 1978
Venue: Monumental Stadium, Buenos Aires
Attendance: 76,609
Referée: Sergio Gonella (ITA)

Just how badly Holland were affected by the pre-match shenanigans which marred the 1978 final against Argentina is debatable, but the unnecessary ten-minute delay while Rene van der Kerkhof was obliged to cover up the protective cast on his wrist benefited no-one but the hosts. But then this was always destined to be Argentina's year. Having survived an early onslaught by the Dutch, the Argentines opened the scoring in the 37th minute when Ardiles threaded a ball through to Kempes who prodded it past Jongbloed. After that, the hosts sat back, content to commit a series of fouls and handballs safe in the knowledge that the weak Italian referee would do nothing to punish them.

It is testament to the determination and skill of the Dutch that they not only equalised – Nanninga heading home Rene van der Kerkhof's cross in the 82nd minute – but were denied a last-gasp victory when Resenbrink's shot came back off the post.

In extra-time the leggy Kempes struck again, galloping into the box and scoring from a rebound of his own shot. Ten minutes later, Bertoni applied the *coup de grâce*, as the weary Dutch failed to clear their lines. Argentina had won the World Cup, but few friends. For the second successive time the trophy had gone to the host nation, and for the second time the bridesmaids had been the Dutch.

ARGENTINA: Fillol, Olguin, Tarantini, Gallego, Galvan, Passarella (c), Bertoni, Ardiles [Larosa 65], Luque, Kempes, Ortiz [Houseman 74]
HOLLAND: Jongbloed, Krol (c), Brandts, Poortvliet, Jansen [Suurbier 72], Haan, R van der Kerkhof, Neeskens, Rep [Nanninga 59], W van der Kerkhof, Rensenbrink

1982

ITALY (0) 3
Rossi 56, Tardelli 68, Altobelli 80
WEST GERMANY (0) 1
Breitner 83

Date: 11 July 1982
Venue: Bernabeu Stadium, Madrid
Attendance: 90,089
Referee: Arnaldo Coelho (BRA)

Italy's convincing and wholly deserved win belied the fact that they had, up until the second- group stage been wholly unconvincing and deserving only of the first plane back to Rome. The moment of epiphany came against the favourites Brazil, when Paolo Rossi bagged a hat-trick in a dramatic 3–2 win and suddenly anything seemed possible.

West Germany, meanwhile, had won few friends on their way to the final. They had adopted a physical approach, personified by the hulking former decathlete Hans Pieter Briegel in midfield and by goalkeeper Harald Schumacher's brutal assault on Battiston in the semi-final against France.

In the end, Briegel's chief contribution in the final was to give away a penalty after 24 minutes which Cabrini scuffed horribly wide. In the second half, he was chasing shadows as the nimble Conti and Tardelli increased the pressure to breaking point. Rossi continued his scoring spree with a close-range header on 53 minutes and then twelve minutes later Marco Tardelli's drive from the edge of the box was surpassed only by his impassioned goal celebration. The ragged Germans were beaten long before Altobelli rounded Schumacher to make it 3–0, but were still able to strike a note of defiance three minutes later when Breitner, in his third World Cup, became only the third player to score in two finals. The defeat was West Germany's first to a European country since 1978.

ITALY: Zoff (c), Bergomi, Cabrini, Gentile, Oriali, Collovati, Scirea, Tardelli, Conti, Rossi, Graziani [Altobelli 7, Causio 89]
WEST GERMANY: Schumacher, Kaltz, Briegel, B Forster, K-H Forster, Stielike, Littbarski, Dremmler [Hrubesch 62], Breitner, Fischer, Rummenigge (c) [H Muller 70]

1986

ARGENTINA (1) 3
Brown 23, Valdano 56, Burruchaga 85
WEST GERMANY (0) 2
Rummenigge 74, Voller 82

Date: 29 June 1986
Venue: Azteca Stadium, Mexico
Attendance 114,580
Referee: Romualdo Arppi (Brazil)

West German coach Franz Beckenbauer admitted before the game that he didn't have the players to win the title – but German football has always been more about solidarity than individual flair, and in 1986 the Kaiser's men came within a whisker of causing a major upset against Maradona's Argentina.

Indeed it has been argued that had it not been for an inexplicable lapse in form by the consistently excellent Schumacher in the German goal, the game might have been won easily.

As it was, two errors by the shaggy-haired keeper gave Argentina a 2–0 lead out of nothing. First he came and missed Burruchaga's free-kick to allow Brown to head into an empty net; then he dithered as Valdano burst through to slot the ball past his right hand.

Two corners in eight minutes by Brehme brought the West Germans level. On 74 minutes Rummenigge, playing through injury, bundled the ball home at the back post, then on 82 Voller got ahead of Pumpido's fists to divert the ball into the net.

Perhaps aware of Rummenigge's condition, Beckenbauer ordered his men to go for the kill instead of playing for extra-time. It was to be a fatal decision. Maradona, largely anonymous until then, played a sublime defence-splitter to put Buruchaga away. Once again Schumacher stayed on his line, and once again he was forced to pick the ball out of the back of the net.

It was harsh on the Germans but, considering the 1986 tournament had been a succession of Maradona masterclasses, the result seemed only fair.

ARGENTINA: Pumpido, Cuciuffo, Olarticoechea, Enrique, Ruggeri, Brown, Giusti, Battista, Burruchaga [Trobbiani 89], Maradona (c), Valdano
WEST GERMANY: Schumacher, Berthold, Briegel, Jakobs, Forster, Eder, Matthaus, Brehme, Allofs [Voller HT], Magath [Hoeness 61], Rummenigge (c)

1990

WEST GERMANY (0) 1
Brehme pen 84
ARGENTINA (0) 0

Date: 8 July 1990
Venue: Olympic Stadium, Rome
Attendance: 73,603
Referee: Edgardo Codesal (MEX)

Perhaps the World Cup was due for a stinker of a final. It certainly got it in 1990. In England, the exploits of Gazza and co. earlier in the tournament tend to overshadow quite what a dismal, mean-spirited game this was.

Argentina were without four suspended players, and were deprived of two more when Monzon and Dezotti were sent off in the second half. Maradona, their inspiration four years earlier, was marked out of the game by the hulking Buchwald.

It made little difference. The Germans, who had scored only a single goal in their previous three matches, rarely came close through open play and the game would have surely drifted into extra-time and most probably penalties had Sensini not brought Voller down in the box with six minutes to go.

One thing the West Germans had proved they were good at in this tournament was penalties (just ask England in the semi-finals), and Andreas Brehme duly converted the spot kick.

It was third time lucky for West Germany, and the last time they would compete as a divided nation. It was just a shame such a momentous occasion should turn out to be such a travesty of a football match.

WEST GERMANY: Illgner, Berthold [Reuter 73], Brehme, Buchwald, Kohler, Augenthaler, Hassler, Matthaus (c), Littbarski, Voller, Klinsmann
ARGENTINA: Goycochea, Simon, Sensini, Basualdo, Serrizuela, Ruggeri [Monzon HT], Burruchaga [Calderon 53], Troglio, Lorenzo, Maradona (c), Dezotti
Sent off: Monzon 64, Dezotti 86

1994

BRAZIL 0
ITALY 0
Brazil 3–2 pens (AET)

PENALTY SHOOT-OUT: Baresi shot over, Marcio Santos saved, Albertini 1–0, Romario 1–1, Evani 2–1, Branco 2–2, Massaro saved, Dunga 2–3, R Baggio shot over.
Date: 17 July 1994
Venue: Rose Bowl, Pasadena
Attendance: 94,194
Referee: Sandor Puhl (HUN)

After the horrors of the 1990 final, we were due something special – and who better to provide it than Brazil and Italy, old adversaries and combatants in the legendary 1970 final?

But the game was another wash-out, the first to be decided on a penalty shoot-out. What chances there were could be counted on one hand, and most of them were for Brazil. Mazinho should have scored when Pagliuca saved Branco's free-kick, Romario missed an open goal and Pagliuca fumbled Mauro Silva's shot onto the post.

For Italy, Roberto Baggio should have scored when put through against Taffarel, but his weary shot betrayed a striker who was both unfit and out of form.

Worse was to come for Baggio as he stepped up to take his penalty. Needing to score to level the scores at 3–3 and keep the shoot-out alive, the pony-tailed Juventus star blazed his shot high over the bar.

The trophy was Brazil's again after 24 years.

BRAZIL: Taffarel, Jorginho [Cafu 21], Branco, Mazinho, Aldair, Marcio Santos, Mauro Silva, Dunga (c), Romario, Bebeto, Zinho [Viola 105] ITALY: Pagliuca, Mussi [Apolloni 34], Benarrivo, Berti, Maldini, Baresi (c), Donadoni, Albertini. Massaro, R Baggio, D Baggio [Evani 94]

1998

FRANCE (2) 3
Zidane 27, 44, Petit 90
BRAZIL (0) 0

Date: 12 July 1998
Venue: Stade de France, Paris
Attendance: 75,000
Referee: Said Belqola (MOR)

After dominating European football for more than two years, France won their first World Cup on home soil and in some style. Architect of their victory was the incomparable Zinedine Zidane, who throughout the tournament had shown a level of skill and technique worthy of the great Brazilians of the past.

By comparison, Brazil's own maestro, Ronaldo, was in disarray. Afflicted by a mystery illness on the day of the game, the predatory striker was initially withdrawn from the starting line-up, only to be reinstated 45 minutes before kick-off.

Quite simply it was one-way traffic. Guivarc'h should have scored twice in the opening minutes as the French laid siege to the Brazilian goal, and had Djorkaeff made contact with his head rather than his shoulder to a near-post cross Taffarel would have had no chance.

As it was, the French crowd had to wait 27 minutes for the first goal. Petit's perfectly flighted corner was met powerfully by Zidane whose header crashed into the back of the net.

With Brazil reeling against the ropes, France went for the kill. In injury time at the end of the first half, Zidane struck again, stooping to head home Djorkaeff's corner from the right.

In the second half, Ronaldo stirred – but was clearly out of sorts. Put through against Barthez, he fluffed the sort of chance he would normally have gobbled up and the goalkeeper collected easily. All around the pitch, Brazilian heads dropped. Even when Desailly was sent off for scything down Cafu after 67 minutes, the South Americans were unable to raise their game.

The *coup de grâce* came in the final seconds of the match when Petit raced clear and coolly slotted the ball past Taffarel to make it 3–0 and send the whole of France into paroxysms of delight.

FRANCE: Barthez, Thuram, Leboeuf, Desailly, Lizarazu, Karembeu [Boghossian 57], Deschamps (c), Zidane, Petit, Djorkaeff (Vieira 76), Guivarc'h [Dugarry 65]

BRAZIL: Taffarel, Cafu, Aldair, Junior Baiano, Roberto Carlos, Leonardo [Denilson 46], Cesar Sampaio [Edmundo 74], Dunga (c), Rivaldo, Ronaldo, Bebeto

2002

BRAZIL (0) 2
Ronaldo 67, 79
GERMANY (0) 0

Date: 30 June 2002
Venue: International Stadium, Yokohama
Attendance: 69,029
Referee: Pierluigi Collina (ITA)

Four years after being waylaid by a mystery illness, Ronaldo was back on the biggest stage in football – and this time he did not disappoint. Two goals – the first a poacher's special, the second a piece of finishing excellence – gave Brazil their fifth World Cup trophy and squashed any speculation that the South Americans were a spent force in world football.

It was Germany, appearing in their fifth final in 18 years, who started the brighter. Inspired by Bernd Schneider, they pressurised the Brazilian goal without ever creating a clear-cut chance, and for a while the final seemed to be heading the same way as it had in France four years earlier.

Brazil, though, looked sharp on the break. Twice Ronaldo was sent clear by the livewire Ronaldinho, only to blow the chance on both occasions. Germany's failure to convert pressure into goals cost them dear in the second half. On 67 minutes a speculative shot from Rivaldo was spilled by the usually rock-solid Kahn in the German goal, and Ronaldo was on hand to bang home the rebound.

Twelve minutes later, Kahn was helpless in the face of some overdue Brazilian magic. Kleberson broke down the right and squared the ball to Rivaldo. Rivaldo stepped over the ball, allowing it to run through to Ronaldo on the edge of the box. There was still much to do, but the striker's finish was emphatic and unstoppable.

Brazil were World Champions again and Ronaldo had silenced the doubters after four years.

BRAZIL: Marcos, Edmilson, Lucio, Roque Junior, Cafu (c), Kleberson, Gilberto, Roberto Carlos, Ronaldinho [Juninho Paulista 85], Rivaldo, Ronaldo [Denilson 90]
GERMANY: Kahn(c), Linke, Ramelow, Metzelder, Frings, Schneider, Jeremies [Asamoah 77], Hamann, Bode [Ziege 84], Neuville, Klose [Bierhoff 73]

2006

FRANCE 1
Zidane 7
ITALY 1
Materazzi 19
Italy 5–3 pens (AET)

PENALTY SHOOT-OUT: Pirlo 1-0, Wiltord 1-1, Materazzi 2-1, Trezeguet hit the crossbar, De Rossi 3-1, Abidal 3-2, Del Piero 4-2, Sagnol 4-3, Grosso 5-3.
Date: 9 July 2006
Venue: Olympiastadion, Berlin
Attendance: 69.000
Referee: Horacio Elizondo (ARG)

The 2006 final will forever be remembered for all the wrong reasons. A moment of madness from one of the most talented players ever to take to the pitch marred an encounter in which both teams initially attacked with gusto, playing with much more open styles than pundits had predicted.

There was excitement early on, with both sides scoring early in the first half. France were awarded a controversial penalty in the 7th minute when Malouda fell in the box after Materazzi appeared to catch his foot. Inevitably, playing in his last match before his official retirement, France captain Zinedine Zidane stepped up to the spot to convert with a casual strike that somewhat fortuitously glanced in off the underside of the crossbar. Italy rallied however and equalised in the 19th minute when Milan's Andrea Pirlo whipped in a corner from the right. Materazzi thumped a header past Fabien Barthez, atoning for his earlier error. The Italian would have a bigger part still to play though.

France found it difficult to deal with set pieces, and indeed, Materazzi saw a second header from another Pirlo corner cleared off the line by Lilian Thuram, before Luca Toni nodded onto the bar – again from a Pirlo corner. Having just held on, France emerged revitalised for the second half, with Thierry Henry at the centre of things. In the 53rd minute Malouda again went down in the box after a Zambrotta tackle, but no penalty was given. Somewhat against the run of play Italy managed to put the ball in the net for a second time; Luca Toni heading in a Pirlo free-kick, but the goal was disallowed for offside. At the other end Henry's running continued to be effective and Buffon showed his quality in saving a snap-shot. Still 1-1 after 90 minutes, the game entered extra time and Malouda was only dispossessed by a last-ditch Cannavaro tackle before Franck Ribery shot wide and Buffon crucially tipped a Zidane header over.

Then, with 10 minutes left of extra time, Zidane and Materazzi looked to exchange words after some shirt-pulling. Having initially walked away, Zidane then stopped, turned around and headbutted Materazzi full in the chest. Materazzi dropped to the floor and although play was halted, Argentinian referee Horacio Elizondo did not appear to have seen the incident. Some minutes elapsed before Zidane was shown a red card in the 110th minute, the referee having apparently been informed of the headbutt by the fourth official via his headset. Zidane trudged from the pitch, ignoring the World Cup trophy displayed next to the tunnel – a picture that dominated the sporting papers the following day. A shell-shocked France managed to hold on without their captain to take the final to penalties.

All five Italy players scored thir spot kicks, and France ultimately lost out when David Trezeguet's penalty hit the crossbar. Fabio Grosso coolly slotted home to make the score 5-3 and secure the World Cup for Italy, the nation's fourth overall.

The fallout from the Zidane incident was huge, and both players were ultimately fined by FIFA. The media clamoured to know what Materazzi had said to Zidane; it later transpired that Zidane had firstly responded to the Italian's shirt-pulling by remarking, 'If you want my shirt, I will give it to you afterwards', and Materazzi retorted, 'Preferisco la puttana di tua sorella' ('I prefer the whore that is your sister'). A nasty insult, certainly, but, the world questioned, did it merit the headbutt that tainted Zidane's incomparable career and may have cost France the World Cup?

FRANCE: Barthez, Sagnol, Thuram, Gallas, Abidal, Vieira [Alou Diarra 56], Makelele, Ribery [Trezeguet 100], Zidane (c), Malouda, Henry [Wiltord 107]
ITALY: Buffon, Zambrotta, Cannavaro (c), Materazzi, Grosso, Gattuso, Pirlo, Camoranesi [Del Piero 86], Perrotta [De Rossi 61], Totti [Iaquinta 61], Toni

⚜ DOGGED GREAVES ⚜

Despite being one of the finest marksmen in the domestic game and scoring 44 goals in 57 appearances for England, Jimmy Greaves's World Cup exploits are perhaps best forgotten as, having secured a place in Alf Ramsey's 1966 team he was injured in the last first-round game against France and, having recovered, was then left out of the final in favour of Geoff Hurst. Indeed Greavesie's finest moment in the white of England may well have come in 1962 during a match against Brazil in Vina Del Mar. Trailing 3–1 and heading out of the World Cup, England's mood was lightened slightly when a dog ran onto the pitch and proceeded to evade all attempts to capture it. Quick as a flash, Greaves got down on all fours in the centre-circle and, by growling at it, succeeded in startling the dog long enough to grab it. It was perhaps symptomatic of Greavesie's England career that, as he carried it to the touchline, the dog urinated all over his England shirt.

⚓ ALF'S PREDICTION ⚓

'Most certainly England will win the World Cup.'
– Alf Ramsey, England manager, on the eve of the 1966 World Cup

⚓ CONDITIONS ⚓

Alf Ramsey only took the England manager's job on condition that the FA selection committee, which picked the team and had done so much to hinder his predecessor Walter Winterbottom, was disbanded.

⚓ WINGLESS WONDERS? ⚓

Alf Ramsey's 1966 England side became known as the Wingless Wonders, but in fact Ramsey used wingers right up until the quarter-final against Argentina.

⚓ PELÉ SPEAKS OUT ⚓

'There is only one way to describe Brazil's 1966 World Cup effort and that is to declare openly that from the beginning it was a total and unmitigated disaster. I suppose our directors put their faith in the old dictum that "God is a Brazilian" – forgetting that God also helps those who help themselves.'
– The great Pelé despairs after Brazil lost to Hungary and Portugal and failed to qualify for the quarter-finals

⚓ ENGLAND PLAYERS WHO PLAYED IN THE 1966 ⚓ TOURNAMENT– BUT NOT IN THE FINAL

Terry Paine (vs Mexico)
Ian Callaghan (vs France)
John Connelly (vs Uruguay)
Jimmy Greaves (vs Uruguay, Mexico, France)

⚓ MEXICO OR BUST ⚓

In 1970 Jimmy Greaves was judged too old, at 30, for a place in the England World Cup squad and was left at home by Sir Alf Ramsey. Greaves, however, had other ideas, and together with rally driver Tony Falls he entered the inaugural World Cup Rally Championship, a race from Wembley to Mexico City covering 16,241 miles and crossing 25 countries. They made it in just under a month. The race, strangely enough, was started by Sir Alf Ramsey.

⚓ THE LONG AND THE SHORT OF IT ⚓

The Group C match between Brazil and China in 2002 featured that particular World Cup's tallest and shortest players – Brazilian midfielder Juninho Paulista at 5ft 4ins (1.67m) and Chinese goalkeeper Jin Jiang, 6ft 4ins (1.98m).

⚖ TRAGIC END ⚖

Georgi Asparoukhov and Stojan Kotkov, who played together for Bulgaria in the 1966 World Cup, were both killed in the same car crash in 1971.

⚖ ARGENTINA TACTICS ⚖

England players recall the brutal quarter-final against Argentina in 1966:

'At any moment, for no reason, you thought you might be attacked from behind.' – Geoff Hurst

'They did tug your hair, spit at you, poke you in the eye and kick you when the ball was miles away and no-one was looking.' – Bobby Moore

'Apart from the violence, I came through with no problems.' – Nobby Stiles

⚖ RATTIN GETS HIS MARCHING ORDERS ⚖

West German referee Rudolf Kreitlein had already booked five players during the stormy World Cup quarter-final between England and Argentina in 1966 when, with nearly half an hour gone, his patience finally snapped. During that time, Argentine skipper Antonio Rattin had spat in front of him, disputed every decision made against his side and committed a series of blatant fouls. Kreitlein, who had already cautioned Rattin, now sent him off. Or at least he tried to. Rattin refused to go, claiming – nonsensically – that he required an interpreter. Meanwhile team-mate Albrecht signalled that if the captain was going then the rest of the side should go with him. The rest of the team, meanwhile, had surrounded the referee and there would be eight minutes of mayhem before Rattin finally left the pitch. Even then it took a quiet word from the police to persuade him to move away from the touchline and begin a long, leisurely walk around the perimeter to the changing rooms.

⚓ VILLAIN OF THE PIECE ⚓

Having already had their captain Antonio Rattin sent off, Argentina cemented their reputation as pantomime villains of the 1966 World Cup after Geoff Hurst gave England a 77th minute lead at Wembley. A small boy ran onto the pitch to congratulate the West Ham striker – but left in tears after Argentine winger Mas clipped him round the ear.

⚓ NO LAUGHING MATTER ⚓

Dick Nanninga of Holland became the first substitute to be sent off in a World Cup tournament when he was given his marching orders in the group match against West Germany in 1978. His offence? Laughing at Uruguayan referee Ramon Barreto. Nanninga would return in the final and score Holland's only goal against Argentina, again as substitute.

⚓ TWO GOALS FOR ERNIE ⚓

The game between Holland and Italy in the second group stage of the 1978 World Cup will be remembered for Arie Haan's 40-yard thunderbolt which beat Dino Zoff off the post. But the match was fairly eventful for Haan's team-mate Ernie Brandts, who put Italy in front with an own goal after nineteen minutes, only to make amends by equalising with a 20-yarder four minutes after the break. He was the first player to score for both sides in a World Cup tournament.

⚓ FOUL PLAY ⚓

There is no love lost between Brazil and Argentina. In their 1978 clash, there were no fewer than seventeen fouls in the first ten minutes. Amazingly no-one was sent off as the two sides ground out a dour 0–0 draw.

⚓ LUQUE PLAYS ON ⚓

Despite the death of his brother in a car crash midway through the 1978 tournament, Argentina's Leopoldo Luque decided to play on in his honour.

⚓ LONG RANGE ⚓

In the 1978 finals in Argentina, the four goals conceded by Italy's Dino Zoff were all shots hit from outside the penalty area.

⚓ GOAL-CRAZY GERMANS ⚓

West Germany were firm favourites, along with Brazil, to win the 1982 World Cup in Spain. Not only were they the reigning European champions, but they had won all eight of their qualifying games, scoring 33 goals and conceding just three. In their first match of the tournament, they lost 2–1 to 1000–1 outsiders Algeria.

⚓ TEUTONIC REVENGE? ⚓

There were red faces all round when Algeria beat West Germany in Group 2 of the 1982 finals. But the Germans were to have their revenge in the most controversial of circumstances eight days later. Algeria led Chile 3–0 at half-time in their last match and, had the score remained the same, only a 4–3 win or better against Austria would have saved the Germans from ignominious elimination. Agonisingly, Chile scored two in the second half – which meant a 1–0 win for West Germany would suffice for them and Austria to proceed on goal difference at Algeria's expense. Because the Algeria match kicked off earlier, the Germans and the Austrians knew this as well. And when Hrubesch scored after eleven minutes, the game deteriorated to the level of a friendly training match, with neither side exerting themselves or showing much interest in scoring again. Furious Algerian fans showed their displeasure by waving banknotes through the wire fencing as the two European sides tamely played out time. Afterwards rumours were rife that the match had been fixed, that the West Germans had reached an agreement with their neighbours to get Algeria eliminated. The counter-argument was that Austria had a long-standing grudge with Germany and therefore had no reason to let them through. Whatever the truth, the match left a sour taste in the mouth as Algeria, who had thrilled the neutrals, were knocked out on goal difference.

Algeria understandably complained to FIFA that the game had been fixed, and called for both sides to be disqualified. Showing a sadly typical lack of backbone, FIFA declined to act. Austria, having spurned a great opportunity to dump their great European rivals out of the World Cup, were themselves expelled in the next stage. West Germany went on to the final where they were well beaten 3–1 by Italy.

⚓ IRISH EYES SMILING ⚓

When Patrick Healy of Coleraine came on as a 77th minute substitute for Northern Ireland in their 1982 group match against Honduras he became the only Irish player in World Cup history to still be playing for an Irish club.

⚓ UNWELCOME RECORD ⚓

Mal Donaghy of Northern Ireland was the first British player to be sent off during World Cup finals when he was dismissed after fouling Camacho of Spain in their 1982 group match. It didn't prevent the ten-man Irish from recording a famous 1–0 win against the hosts.

⚓ SOLIDARITY ⚓

There was more at stake than just a football match when Poland played USSR in 1982. Back home the Poles, in the form of trade union Solidarity, were protesting vociferously against their Soviet overlords – and in Barcelona's Nou Camp stadium dozens of *Solidarnosc* flags were draped on the terraces. That was until the Spanish police waded in with batons raised to remove the banners, apparently at the request of Soviet television. It was a shameful incident and one which only served to raise the profile of the union to the watching millions. The game itself ended in a tame 0–0 draw.

⚓ KEV AND TREV ⚓

Injured before the tournament, Kevin Keegan and Trevor Brooking were finally pressed into emergency service 63 minutes into England's crunch match against hosts Spain in 1982. Needing to win by at least two goals, Brooking fired a shot straight at goalkeeper Arkonada and Keegan missed a far-post header ('No excuses – I should have buried it.'). England were out and neither Keegan and Brooking would play for their country again. Sadly the World Cup careers of these brilliant players amounted to just 27 minutes.

⚓ TV INFLUENCE ⚓

The influence of TV companies in shaping World Cup tournaments was never more in evidence than in Mexico in 1986. It was ordered that matches had to end precisely after 90 minutes to fit in with advertising schedules, while kick-offs were brought forward to lunchtime – the hottest part of the day – to enable matches to be screened at convenient times in Europe. Chief culprit for this lunatic scheduling – which would be repeated in the USA in 1994 – was Guillermo Canedo, a FIFA vice-president who also happened to be a leading executive with an independent Mexican television company responsible for networking the coverage. When asked about the prohibitively high ticket prices, Canedo replied that 'people always have TV'.

⚓ THE RIGHT CHOICE ⚓

Enzo Scifo was qualified to play for Italy in the 1986 World Cup, but instead chose to play for his native Belgium. It proved to be the right choice, as Scifo, one of the stars of the tournament, guided the unfancied Belgians through to the last four while Italy failed to even make the quarter-finals.

⚓ NOBBY'S NIGHTMARE ⚓

England cruised to victory in their final 1966 Group 1 game against France. But while Roger Hunt celebrated his 28th birthday by scoring both goals, team-mate Nobby Stiles had a match to forget. Booked for a foul and then extremely lucky not to have been sent off for a late challenge on Simon, his misery was compounded when he was accidentally knocked flying by the referee. Indeed there were many FA officials who wanted Stiles dropped from the team. Fortunately, Alf Ramsey held firm – and the rest is history.

⚓ LONG SERVANT ⚓

At the age of 37 Mexico's goalkeeper Antonio Carbajal was recalled to the side for their final 1966 group match against Uruguay. Remarkably it was his fifth World Cup finals, a record at the time – and he celebrated by keeping a clean sheet.

⚓ THE LONG WAIT ⚓

Ian Callaghan of Liverpool played only once in the 1966 World Cup finals, against Mexico. The next time he played for England was in 1977, a gap of 11 years 59 days – still the England record.

⚓ SWISS SHOOT THEMSELVES IN THE FOOT ⚓

Having arrived at the 1966 World Cup as rank outsiders, the Swiss did nothing to help their own cause by suspending their two best players, Werner Leimgruber and Jakob Kuhn. The two players had broken a curfew and were sidelined on the eve of the first match against Germany – a match which they subsequently lost 5–0. It was to be Switzerland's last appearance in a World Cup until 1994.

⚓ NOT A NATIONAL ⚓

Eusebio, star of the Portugal side in 1966, was born in Mozambique.

⚓ UNPARALLELED ADEMIR ⚓

Eight years before the arrival of Pelé, Brazilian football was in thrall to another gifted genius. Ademir entranced the opposition in 1950, and none more so than Sweden against whom he scored four brilliant goals in a 7–1 rout. Pick of the bunch was his third, in which he trapped the ball between his ankles and jumped over the diving goalkeeper before slotting it coolly into the back of the net.

⚓ UP STEPS O'LEARY ⚓

On a night of almost unbearable tension in Genoa, the Republic of Ireland and Romania went to penalties in a match to decide who would progress to the 1990 quarter-finals. With the scores tied at 4–4, veteran keeper Pat Bonner dived to his right to save Timofte's timid kick – which meant that the fate of the Irish lay with defender David O'Leary, a man who had never taken a penalty in competitive football. O'Leary stepped up and calmly slotted the spot-kick, sparking wild scenes of jubilation among the Irish fans and guaranteeing their highest-ever World Cup finish.

⚲ MUSICAL URUGUAY ⚲

Schubert Gambetta played in defence for Uruguay in 1950, while Mozart Javier was a midfielder in a qualifying match against England in 1977.

⚲ QUITE A DEBUT ⚲

Ruben Moran is the only player to make his international debut in a World Cup final. He appeared on the wing for Uruguay in the deciding group match in 1950 and helped his team to a famous 2–1 win over the much-fancied Brazilians in Rio.

⚲ FAULTLESS WYSSLING DISPLAY ⚲

Two of the referees in the 1954 World Cup finals were Paul Wyssling of Switzerland and Charlie Faultless of Scotland.

⚲ LEG MASSAGE ⚲

Having already lost 12–0 to the same side at the 1952 Olympics, the South Koreans knew it was going to be a long afternoon when Hungary's Puskas scored after just 11 minutes of their Group 2 match at the 1954 World Cup in Switzerland. When Peter Palotas slid home the seventh with thirteen minutes still remaining, it was too much for South Korea's 37-year-old midfielder Chung Nam-sik who sat down exhausted on the pitch. Fortunately, Hungarian defender Jeno Buzanszky was on hand to revive the veteran with a timely leg massage. It didn't stop the rout, however – Palotas and Puskas scored twice more to complete a 9–0 hammering for the Koreans.

⚲ GERMAN STUDS ⚲

In 1954, the West Germans were the first team to use screw-in studs.

⚓ VAIN HOPE ⚓

'What's to stop us beating Uruguay?'
– Scotland captain Willie Cunningham on the eve of their 7–0 hiding by Uruguay in the 1954 World Cup

⚓ HARD EFFORT ⚓

'Willie Cunningham got a sunburned tongue trying to contain Ghiggia.'
– Scotland's Tommy Docherty reflects on his captain's vain efforts during his side's 7–0 defeat to Uruguay in 1954

⚓ PURPLE PROSE ⚓

'Not just a defeat – a disaster!'
– headline in an Italian newspaper after the *Azzurri* crashed 4–0 against the hosts Switzerland in 1954

⚓ A GREAT RECORD ENDS ⚓

West Germany's 3–2 win over Hungary in the 1954 final brought to an end a run of 29 matches without defeat. During that time, Hungary – with Puskas, Hidegkuti and Kocsis to the fore – had beaten Czechoslovakia 5–0, Italy 5–1, Sweden 6–2, South Korea 12–0 and 9–0, and England 6–3 and 7–1. They would never again reach such a pinnacle. Two years later, the Soviet Union invaded Hungary, and what remained of the Magic Magyars scattered to clubs elsewhere in Europe.

⚓ LAGER LOUT ⚓

Helmut Rahn of West Germany who had scored twice in the 1954 final aganst Hungary also scored two goals in his country's 3–1 win over Argentina in the opening game of the 1958 World Cup in Sweden and went on to score six in total as the Germans progressed as far as the semi-finals. But the influential striker only made the squad at the very last after coach Sepp Herberger persuaded him to lose weight by reducing his lager intake.

⊥ THE DAY AFTER ⊥

Wales' 1958 World Cup tie against Hungary was played on 17 June. The previous day Imre Nagy, leader of the 1956 uprising, had been executed and as a result the game was played to an eerie background of Free Hungarian chanting and banners draped in black. For the record, Wales won 2–1.

⊥ ITALIAN AT HEART ⊥

Mazzola – whose real name was José Altafini – played up front for Brazil in the 1958 World Cup finals, and took his name from the great Italian Valentino Mazzola who was killed in the 1949 air crash which wiped out the entire Torino squad. The nineteen-year-old clearly had an affinity for Italy, because he moved there after the World Cup and played for them in the 1962 tournament. Valentino's son, Sandro Mazzola played in three World Cups for Italy.

⊥ WRONG DIAGNOSIS ⊥

For their final group game against the USSR in 1958, Brazilian coach Vicente Feola decided to blood two promising untested players, one a teenager. Before the game, he asked the team psychiatrist Joao Carvalhaes what he thought of them. The first, said Carvalhaes, was 'too young, too infantile' and the other 'so unsophisticated that including him in the team would be a disaster'. Feola disagreed and picked the tyros anyway. Their names? Pelé and Garrincha.

⊥ DON'T WORRY ⊥

'If I were Svensson, I wouldn't worry about this.'
– commentator Kenneth Wolstenholme with some words of consolation for the Swedish goalkeeper after Pelé had just scored a sublime goal to put Brazil 3–1 ahead in the World Cup final of 1958

⚑ OUT OF CONTROL ⚑

The award for weakest refereeing performance of all time surely goes to Albert Dusch of West Germany, who was put in charge of the 1962 group match between USSR and Yugoslavia. There was little love lost between the two sides, as became apparent from the start when both sides launched into each other with a series of fouls. At the very least a warning might have calmed the situation, but Dusch did nothing. The situation reached farcical proportions when USSR's Dubinsky was hospitalised with a broken leg following a horrendous tackle by Yugoslav skipper Muhamed Mujic. The challenge was so bad, Mujic was later sent home by his own management – but again Dusch did nothing. Nor did he react when struck in the face by Yugloslav forward Jerkovic. USSR eventually won 2–0, but by then the game was totally out of control. Unsurprisingly, it was the first and last World Cup game refereed by Herr Dusch.

⚑ THANKS, LADS! ⚑

The vituperative Italian press have always been quick to attack their own players, and often with good cause. But in 1962 Giovanni Ferrari's men had good reason to feel aggrieved with their coverage. Shortly before the tournament, two Italian journalists had published an excoriating attack on the host nation Chile, emphasising the poverty of Santiago, the corruption of the government and the dubious nocturnal activities of the local women. Not surprisingly, the Italian football team was greeted with a torrent of abuse whenever it took the field during the tournament, not least during the match against Chile when they were kicked and spat at. The Italians were knocked out in the first round and were no doubt relieved – until they returned home to find themselves lambasted by the Italian media for not performing.

⚑ STATING THE OBVIOUS ⚑

'They were very weak and had no training.'
– Hungary's Ferenc Puskas following his side's 9–0 demolition of South Korea in 1954

⚱ GRATEFUL PELÉ ⚱

The 1962 Group 3 match between Brazil and Czechoslovakia ended 0–0, and the closest the South Americans came to a goal was in the opening minutes when Pelé sliced through the defence and hit the post. In doing so, the 21-year-old genius aggravated a groin injury and was forced to spend the rest of the match lurking ineffectively on the wing. It was the end of his tournament, but the great man recalled later how Czech defenders Popluhar and Lala refused to go into any hard tackles whenever Pelé got the ball. 'It was one of those things I shall always remember with emotion, and one of the finest things that happened in my football career,' he said.

⚱ MEXICO AT LAST ⚱

On 7 June 1962, at the El Tranque stadium in Viña Del Mar, Chile, Mexico beat Czechoslovakia 3–1. Astonishingly, it was their 14th attempt to win a finals match and it was done despite conceding a goal after just fifteen seconds.

⚱ WORST INTERNATIONAL ⚱

'We would have a dozen passes at our end and then try and hit the ball up to our one forward. He was bound to lose it. So they had a dozen passes down their end. It was one of the worst internationals of all time.'
– Bobby Moore's verdict on England's dismal 0–0 draw against Bulgaria in Group 4 of the 1962 World Cup in Chile

⚱ GAME OVER ⚱

'Even though we scored after just four minutes, I had the sneaking suspicion that the game was already over. Instead of looking dejected, the Brazilians were calling for the ball to restart the game. If that was their attitude, we were in trouble.'
– Sweden's English coach George Raynor correctly anticipates Pelé-inspired Brazil's 5–2 win in the World Cup final of 1958

⚐ THE ATHLETE AND THE WORLD ⚐

It's only 36 centimetres high, but it is the most famous sporting trophy of all. The World Cup is made of solid, 18-carat gold and weighs 4,970 grams. Two rings of semi-precious malachite stones adorn the base. It was designed by Italian sculptor Silvio Gazzaniga in 1971, following a FIFA competition to design the cup after the Pelé-inspired Brazilians of 1970 took possession of the Jules Rimet Trophy with their third World Cup triumph, a 4-1 victory over Italy in Mexico.

'My inspiration for the design came from two basic elements – the athlete and the world,' Gazzaniga said. 'I had it in my mind to create something that symbolised effort and exertion, while at the same time expressing harmony, simplicity and peace.'

He came up with two celebrating athletes, apparently lifting the world itself in a moment of sublime triumph.

For FIFA, led by its English president Sir Stanley Rous, it was no contest and Gazzaniga beat 52 other designs to win the commission.

The World Cup Trophy

⚓ THE EMPEROR'S NEW CLOTHES ⚓

Franz Beckenbauer was a footballing legend who had made 103 appearances for West Germany, played in three World Cups, two finals and lifted the trophy in 1974. Even so, there were those within the German game who had their doubts when he was made national team coach in 1984. For a start, he had no coaching licence. And, traditionally, the German boss was always succeeded by his qualified assistant. They needn't have worried: in 1986 Beckenbauer took his unfancied team to within an ace of beating Argentina in the final, and four years later in Italy became the second man, after Mario Zagallo, to win the World Cup both as a player and a coach. *Der Kaiser* indeed.

⚓ URUGUAY UNINSPIRING ⚓

Uruguay reached the second round of the 1986 World Cup without winning a game, scoring only one goal and having two players sent off.

⚓ LINEKER HAT-TRICK ⚓

Gary Lineker's three goals against Poland in 1986 made him only the second England player to bag a World Cup hat-trick. The first was Geoff Hurst twenty years earlier.

⚓ FRANCE AT LAST ⚓

When France beat Italy 2–0 in the second round of the 1986 tournament in Mexico, it was the first time they had beaten their European rivals in major tournaments since 1920.

⚓ BRAZIL OUT ⚓

Brazil crashed out of World Cup '86 after a quarter-final penalty shoot-out against France, and were under-standably bemused to be flying home having won four, lost none, scored ten and conceded only one goal in the tournament.

⚑ FLARE-UP ⚑

The World Cup qualifier between Brazil and Chile in 1989 was an explosive match in more ways than one. Played in front of 114,000 screaming fans in Rio, Brazil were leading 1–0 and seemingly cruising to the finals in Italy when, after 69 minutes, a flare was thrown into the Chilean goalmouth. Roberto Rojas, the goalkeeper, fell writhing to the ground, apparently in agony after being struck on the head. The Chilean players refused to continue, claiming that the incident had left them physically and mentally shattered, and the game was abandoned. However, subsequent video footage revealed that the flare had missed Rojas by a mile and that his play-acting was just a cynical ploy to get the Brazilians disqualified. As a result Rojas was banned for life, as were the Chilean officials and medical staff who had happily joined in the con. The match was awarded 2–0 to Brazil, meaning Chile failed to qualify and they were banned from the 1994 tournament for good measure.

⚑ TASTE OF SUCCESS ⚑

The first goal of the 1994 World Cup qualifying campaign was scored on 21 March 1992 by Mark Lugris, a New York restaurant manager, for Puerto Rico against the Dominican Republic.

⚑ ZAMBIA TRAGEDY ⚑

Zambia were one of the emerging powers in African football and firmly expected to do well in the 1994 World Cup finals in America. But, en route from Mauritius to Senegal to compete in a qualifying match on 27 April 1993, the military aircraft in which they were travelling crashed into the ocean off Gabon. Eighteen of the country's top players were killed. The tragedy united the nation and they resolved to continue their qualification bid. Needing just a draw against Morocco to reach the finals, Zambia were beaten 1–0.

⚑ HOME FLOPS ⚑

In 1994 none of the four home nation countries qualified for the World Cup finals, the first time this had happened since they had become eligible to compete. Both Andy Roxburgh of Scotland and Graham Taylor of England resigned as national manager after the failure.

⚓ WITCH DOCTOR ⚓

In an effort to qualify for the 1994 finals in the USA, Zimbabwe employed the services of a witch doctor before their vital match against Cameroon. Zimbabwe lost 3–1.

⚓ THE WRITE STUFF ⚓

Joao Saldanha, a Brazilian journalist, was such a vehement critic of the national side in the aftermath of the 1966 World Cup debacle that the Brazilian FA made the extraordinary decision to call his bluff and make him manager for the 1970 campaign. Unfortunately, Saldanha was better at dishing out criticism than he was at taking it and, after he was arrested at the house of a rival journalist brandishing a revolver, he was swiftly replaced in time for the 1970 tournament by Mario Zagallo, who had starred as a player in the 1958 and 1962 finals.

⚓ SUB SCORES ⚓

Juan Ignacio Basaguren's 83rd-minute goal for Mexico in their 4–0 win over El Salvador in 1970 made him the first substitute to score in a World Cup tournament. He had been on the pitch for just eight minutes.

⚓ HIGH FLYERS ⚓

The Group 2 game between Italy and Sweden in 1970 was played at the Luis Gutierrez Dosal stadium in Toluca, Mexico. At 8,744ft (2,665m) above sea-level it remains the highest World Cup match ever played.

8,744ft (2,665m) above sea level

Luis Gutierrez Dosal Stadium

4,409ft (1,344m) above sea level

Ben Nevis

⚓ CALAMITY JAMES ⚓

If, as the late Brian Clough insisted, it only takes a second to score a goal, then just think what can happen in two minutes. That's how long it took for England goalkeeper David James's world to collapse and for England's 2004 World Cup qualifier against Austria to turn to clay. With 71 minutes gone, Sven's men were leading 2–0 and playing comfortably for the win in Vienna. Then, against the run of play, substitute Ronald Kollmann bent home a free-kick past the stranded James. It was a blow, though not the end of the world – but the goal gave the Austrians renewed confidence and for the next two minutes they launched an assault on the wobbly-looking England defence. Disaster almost inevitably struck: Andreas Ivanschitz struck a speculative-looking shot from the edge of the box which slithered under James's body into the net. England managed to hold on for the draw, but James's days as England's number one keeper were numbered – and what chances he had of being recalled were all but dashed eleven months later when, coming on as substitute during a friendly match against Denmark, he let in four second-half goals and claimed that he hadn't warmed up properly.

⚓ LIECHTENSTEIN ON A ROLL ⚓

It is highly unlikely that Liechtenstein will ever compete in the finals of a World Cup. The tiny principality has a population of just 33,000 and its football team consists of part-timers. Since they began entering World Cup qualifiers in 1998, they have been beaten 11–1 by Macedonia and conceded sixteen goals over two legs against Romania. In fact in 60 internationals, Liechtenstein have only won once – against Azerbaijan. So it was understandable that nobody in their right minds gave them a chance against Portugal when the European Championship runners-up rolled into town for a qualifying match in October 2004. For a while it was a sadly familiar story: Pedro Pauleta scored after 23 minutes, and an own goal by Daniel Hasler meant Liechtenstein were two goals down at half-time. But whatever was said during the interval clearly worked wonders. Three minutes into the second half, Franz Burgmeier stunned the Portuguese with a crisp shot. But this was nothing compared to the shock when Thomas Beck equalised after 76 minutes. The draw earned Liechtenstein their first World Cup qualifying point after twenty defeats in eight years, during which they had scored just four goals and conceded 84. Astonishingly, they then went on to defeat Luxembourg 4–0 in their next qualifying match to record their first win. Sadly, the team has since lapsed into its losing ways once again.

⚓ THE RETURN OF SOCRATES ⚓

In his prime, Brasiliero Sampaio de Souza Vieira de Oliviera – aka Socrates – was the fulcrum of the great Brazil team of 1982. When he retired after the 1986 finals, most people in Britain thought they'd seen the last of this brilliant, elegant midfielder. In November 2004, however, he made a dramatic, not to say astonishing, return – for Garforth Town, of the Northern Counties East League Division One. Garforth's owner-manager Simon Clifford, a successful businessman with contacts in Brazil, managed to persuade 50-year-old Socrates (who was working as a doctor in Sao Paulo) to make a guest appearance against Tadcaster. So it was that on a freezing cold day, with 78 minutes gone and the scores level at 2–2, the great man levered himself off the bench and trotted onto the pitch. In truth, the overweight and greying figure in the number six shirt was unrecognisable as the great player he had been in his slim-hipped prime, and it is estimated that he touched the ball no more than four times in his twelve-minute return to action. But those who were present will never forget the day a Brazilian legend played in the Northern Counties League.

⚓ DRUGGED? ⚓

In 1990 Brazil were beaten 1–0 by Argentina in a tense second-round knockout match in Turin. After the game, Brazil's Branco made the extraordinary claim that he had been drugged by a spiked water bottle handed to him by the Argentines. At the time the claim was dismissed as sour grapes – but then, in December 2004, Diego Maradona, who had been captain of the Argentina side that day, admitted that it was true and that the water bottle contained traces of the 'date-rape' drug Rohypnol. Although FIFA say they are powerless to act on the allegations, the incident has only increased the bitter rivalry between the two South American sides, and added an extra piquancy to all prospective World Cup encounters.

⚓ THE FINAL WORD ⚓

'There is too much bad behaviour in football now. Too much play acting and not enough respect for opponents and the referee. And the international players are treated like babies these days. Everything is done for them. We just had to muddle through on our own. And look what they are paid!'– Lucien Laurent, scorer of the first ever World Cup goal for France against Mexico on 13 July 1930. Lucien died in April 2005 aged 97.

⚐ ROBOCUP ⚐

Nobody knows who will contest the 2050 World Cup – or indeed whether it will be contested by humans at all. In 2003 a team of experts in the field of artificial intelligence announced they were embarking on a major project aimed at creating a team of 'fully autonomous humanoid robots' sufficiently skilled at football to be able to take on and beat the reigning human world champions by 2050.

⚐ SAD SEVENTIES ⚐

For a team which had been top of the world in the 1960s, the 1970s represented a period of unprecedented World Cup failure for England. The team which had been tipped to win the trophy in 1970 failed to even qualify for the finals under Alf Ramsey in 1974 and in 1978 under first Don Revie and then Ron Greenwood respectively. The full, dismal records make painful reading even now:

1974
Wales 0–1 England
England 1–1 Wales
Poland 2–0 England
England 1–1 Poland
(England finish second in the group and are eliminated)

1978
Finland 1–4 England
England 2–1 Finland
Italy 2–0 England
England 5–0 Luxembourg
Luxembourg 0–2 England
England 0–2 Italy
(England finish second in the group and are eliminated)

⚓ ENGLAND'S WORLD CUP FINALS RECORD ⚓

- **Most goals scored in a finals match:** 4 (vs Belgium 1954, vs West Germany 1966)
- **Largest margin of victory:** 3 goals (vs Poland and Paraguay 1986, vs Denmark 2002)
- **Largest margin of defeat:** 2 goals (4–2 vs Uruguay 1954, 3–1 vs Brazil 1962)
- **Number of scoreless draws:** 8 (Brazil 1958, Bulgaria 1962, Uruguay 1966, West Germany and Spain 1982, Morocco 1986, Holland 1990, Nigeria 2002)
- **Most matches in a tournament:** 7 in 1990
- **Fewest matches in a tournament:** 3 in 1954 and 1958
- **Most goals scored in a tournament:** 11 in 1966
- **Fewest goals scored in a tournament:** 2 in 1950

⚓ GREAT GAMES: ARGENTINA 2–2 ENGLAND ⚓ (4–3 AFTER PENALTIES), 1998

Perhaps not so great if you're an England supporter, but without doubt the best game of the 1998 tournament in France. Quite simply, the match had everything. And of course, it has the extra frisson of being between two old rivals who had never buried the hatchet since 1966. There were two spectacular goals by Owen and Zanetti, David Beckham's petulant kick at Simeone which earned him a red card, and then the agonies of yet another failed penalty shoot-out with David Batty's penalty being saved.

⚓ TRAVELLING WITH THE BARE MINIMUM ⚓

England named a 22-man squad for the 1954 tournament in Switzerland, but only seventeen players travelled to Switzerland. The other five squad members were left at home as reserves and were never called to active status. England named a 21-man squad for the 1950 tournament in Brazil, the lowest number they have ever called for a World Cup finals squad, but all players were members of the travelling party.

⚲ A LOAD OF BALLS ⚲

The first official World Cup ball was introduced in 1970 by adidas, and was the now classic 32-panel black and white Telstar ball. The different colours were aimed at making the ball more visible on black and white television sets. A similar Telstar ball was used for the 1974 finals. In 1978 the players used a Tango Durlast, and in 1982 the design was upgraded to make the ball waterproof. This was the last time a genuine leather football was used in the World Cup. The Azteca ball used in 1986 was coated in polyurethane, making it rain-resistant, and by 1994 the Questra ball featured an internal layer of polyurethane foam designed to improve control and also increase acceleration when it was kicked. In 1998 the first coloured ball was used, sporting the red, white and blue tricolour of France printed on an undercoat of syntactic foam. For the 2006 tourmament in Germany, adidas produced the Teamgeist ball, made up of strange propeller-shaped panels 'designed to minimize corners and to create a more homogenous system in terms of performance and look'. The 2010 ball, unveiled in December 2009, is the Jabulani, which means 'to celebrate' or 'to bring joy' in isiZulu, one of the official languages of the host nation, South Africa. The design reflects the unique African spirit and features 11 different colours, representing the 11 players in a football team. adidas say that the ball is the roundest yet, and it also incorporates 'grip n'groove' technology to provide stability and accuracy in flight as well as giving 'more futuristic texture and extensive grip'.

⚲ ALL CHANGE FOR THE REFEREES ⚲

In 1930 the World Cup final between Uruguay and Argentina was refereed by John Langenus of Belgium, who wore a white dress shirt, dinner jacket, necktie and a pair of plus-fours, and who prepared for the big game by sitting down to a slap-up luncheon with other FIFA officials. It's a far cry from the gruelling preparation the referees for the 2006 World Cup finals have been put through. At a special FIFA-organised workshop in February 2005 around 50 hopefuls were subjected to a thorough medical check-up and a number of theoretical and practical training sessions. They were also made to work on their physical fitness before being required to complete a demanding fitness test. For the rest of the year every one of their major matches was scrutinised by members of the FIFA refereeing panel and their performances assessed. The announcement of the final shortlist of World Cup referees was due to be made in the spring of 2006.

⚘ SUCKER PUNCH ⚘

'Most unfancied teams at the World Cup at least have a puncher's chance. But the USA don't even have a puncher.'
– pundit Rodney Marsh, after the USA had been hammered 5–1 by Czechoslovakia in their opening match of the 1990 World Cup

⚘ COSTA RICA RECORD ⚘

Costa Rica's shock 1–0 win over Scotland in the 1990 World Cup finals made them the first team from Central America to win a World Cup match in Europe.

⚘ BROTHERLY LOVE ⚘

In their 1990 first-round match against Colombia, the United Arab Emirates fielded two sets of brothers: Eissa and Ibrahim Meer, and Nasser and Fahad Khamis.

⚘ OVERACTING ⚘

The Colombians have always flattered to deceive at World Cups, and 1990 in Italy was no exception. In fact, during their brief stay, the South Americans quickly became the team everybody loved to hate on account of their constant play-acting. The best moment came in their final group game against West Germany when skipper Carlos Valderrama went down under a non-existent challenge and lay there, writhing in pretend agony, for fully three minutes until he realised that the referee was having none of it. At which point he got up and continued playing.

⚘ THE ITALIANS ARE NOT IMPRESSED ⚘

'No Football, We're English'
– headline in *Gazzetta dello Sport* after England's turgid 1–1 draw with the Republic of Ireland in 1990. Statisticians later calculated that the ball had been in play for only 49 of the 90 minutes

⚓ PLAYING AWAY ⚓

Confined to the island of Sardinia for the duration of the first round of matches during Italia '90, England's players found different ways of relieving the boredom. Indeed Isabella Ciaravolo, their Sardinian liaison officer, was transferred elsewhere after unsubstantiated reports of her liaisons with members of the England squad!

⚓ CHANGE OF EDITORIAL POLICY ⚓

'The *Sun* speaks its mind. Bring them home!'
– editorial after England's 1–1 draw against the Republic of Ireland, 11 June 1990

'We never seriously doubted England's chances of clawing their way through the World Cup field.'
– editorial in the *Sun* after England qualified for the quarter-finals, 26 June 1990

'Around Gazza and his young gang we can build a team to rule the world. Four years on, remember you read it first in the *Sun*!'
– editorial in the *Sun* after England were knocked out on penalties in the semi-final against West Germany, 4 July 1990

⚓ THE HEAT IS ON ⚓

'I would tell those gentlemen of FIFA to take their suits off and play football. If they were to think more about football and less about business there would be night games.'
– Mexico coach Miguel Mejia Baron complains bitterly about FIFA's decision toplay matches during the 1994 finals in the USA in the scorching midday heat in order to maximise television coverage

⚓ CRUSHED ⚓

Tragedy marred the qualifying match between Guatemala and Costa Rica in 1993, when 60,000 people attempted to cram into a stadium with a capacity of just 45,000. In a hideous repeat of the Hillsborough disaster four years earlier, 84 people were asphyxiated against the perimeter fence in the resulting crush.

⚐ THE POLISH CRISIS ⚐

'It's worse than losing a war. It's a national disaster of the highest magnitude.'
– Lord Wigg, after England's draw against Poland in 1973

⚐ MONTEZUMA'S REVENGE? ⚐

Gordon Banks was undoubtedly the best goalkeeper in the world in 1970, as his save against Pelé in the Brazil match proved. But he was also only human – which was why his defences were powerless against an infamous dose of Montezuma's Revenge on the eve of the crunch match against West Germany in Leon. Alf Ramsey, paranoid about foreign food, had brought his own supplies with him. But Banks blamed his suffering on a 'dodgy bottle of Mexican beer'. And suffer he did. From both ends at the same time. Yet on the day of the match, Banks woke feeling much improved. Ramsey took a gamble and included him in the side. Then, shortly before kick off, Banks suffered a relapse. As he retreated to his sick bed, the England boss informed reserve goalkeeper Peter Bonetti that he was in. Perhaps it was not the best preparation for the man known by Chelsea fans as 'The Cat': he was arguably at fault for all three German goals as England squandered a 2–0 lead to be eliminated from the tournament.

⚐ PUPPET ON A STRING ⚐

'He hurled himself arms, knees and bumps-a-daisy all over his penalty area like a slackly-strung marionette. And all with a half-taunting, half-surprised smile which made one think this might be his first ever game.'
– Frank Keating of the *Guardian* describes Poland's keeper Jan Tomaszewski, whose heroics in 1973 denied England a place in the following year's World Cup finals in West Germany

⚐ A VOTE OF NO-CONFIDENCE ⚐

Midway through a 1993 qualifier against Iraq, Saudi Arabia's goalkeeper allowed the ball to trickle through his legs into the net. A watching Royal Prince immediately sent instructions to Saudi Arabia's Brazilian-born coach Jose Candido to substitute the keeper. When he did not, Candido was promptly sacked.

⚓ VOGTS OF NO CONFIDENCE ⚓

'If I said I could walk on water, my accusers would say it is because I cannot swim.'
– German coach Berti Vogts feels the heat after his side's disappointing showing at the 1994 World Cup. And to think he then went on to manage Scotland!

⚓ BOMB THREAT ⚓

Colombia started their 1994 World Cup pool game against the hosts USA without Gabriel Gomes after an unknown terrorist group threatened to blow his family up if he played. Those who thought this was an overreaction were given a salutary lesson in Colombian lawlessness when Andres Escobar – who had the misfortune to score an own goal in the match – was shot dead in Medellin just nine days later.

⚓ EARLY BATH FOR SONG ⚓

Cameroon's seventeen-year-old defender Rigobert Song became the youngest player to be sent off in a World Cup finals match when he was dismissed after 64 minutes of their group game against Brazil in 1994. He was red-carded again four years later against Chile.

⚓ OPRAH TAKES A TRIP AND MISS ROSS MISSES ⚓

The inaugural game in group C of the 1994 World Cup finals was played at Soldier Field in Chicago, and the organisers in the Windy City decided to pull out all the stops by inviting Diana Ross and chat-show queen Oprah Winfrey to appear in the grand opening ceremony. Sadly, things did not go to plan. First Oprah tripped up and went sprawling face first onto the stage. Then, just a few yards out and with an oversized net gaping, Ross somehow contrived to blast the ball wide from a staged penalty. This pre-match entertainment proved far more engaging than the match that followed, with Germany beating Bolivia by a single goal to nil.

⚘ ADIOS ETCHEVERRY ⚘

With ten minutes to go and trailing 1–0 to Germany in their opening pool match of the 1994 World Cup, Bolivia sent on star player Marco Etcheverry for his first game in over eight months following a serious knee injury. Two minutes later, Etcheverry was back in the dug-out having been sent off. He was banned from the next two matches, which effectively meant his World Cup was over.

⚘ NEW IMAGE ⚘

'We need to shake off this Third World image. We are no more willing to see witch doctors on the pitch than cannibals at the refreshment stalls.' – a frustrated member of the African Football Confederation, after Ivory Coast had employed the services of a witch doctor prior to their World Cup qualifier against Nigeria in 1993. Ivory Coast won 2–1

⚘ BUNKING OFF ⚘

At fifteen years, four months and 28 days, Farooq Aziz became the youngest World Cup qualifier player when he appeared for Pakistan in an Asian group qualifier against China in 1993. In order to play, Farooq had to first get permission from his headmaster to take the afternoon off. Pakistan lost 5–0. However, the record was smashed in 2001 when Souleymane Mamam appeared as a substitute for Togo in a qualifying match against Zambia aged 13 years and 310 days old.

⚘ OLD QUALIFIER ⚘

Taylor MacDonald of US Virgin Islands was 46 years and 180 days old when he played against St Kitts & Nevis on 18 February 2004, making him the oldest player ever to appear in a World Cup qualifier.

⚘ RAPID-FIRE SCORING ⚘

Abdelhamid Basuoni holds the record for the fastest World Cup hat-trick outside of the finals when he scored three times in just 177 seconds for Egypt in a qualifier against Namibia in July 2002.

⚓ LITTLE EEL ⚓

Diego Maradona's brilliant second goal against England in the 1986 quarter-final left most people speechless – but not Radio 2 commentator Bryon Butler, whose now-classic description of the goal captured it perfectly:

> '*Maradona turns like a little eel and comes away from trouble … Little squat man … outside Fenwick, leaves him for dead … comes inside Terry Butcher, leaves him for dead … And puts the ball away! … And that is why Maradona is the greatest player in the world!*'

⚓ TIGHT-KNIT SQUAD ⚓

When Brazil won the World Cup in 1962 they did so using just twelve players during the six-match tournament in Chile.

⚓ HOST OF GOOD FORTUNE ⚓

It certainly pays to host a World Cup finals. Since 1930 no host nation has failed to qualify from the first round, and only the USA (1994) and Japan (2002) did not reach the quarter-finals. Of the seventeen tournaments, six have been won by the host nation.

⚓ HITTING THE RIGHT NOTE ⚓

The closing ceremony of the 1990 World Cup in Rome was marked by a 'Century gala' with a performance by the three tenors, Luciano Pavarotti, Plácido Domingo and José Carreras, who are avid soccer fans. It attracted a live audience of 6,000 and 1.5 billion TV viewers worldwide.

⚓ SMALL FRY ⚓

Berne, Switzerland, became the smallest city to host a World Cup final when Hungary and West Germany met each other in front of 62,000 spectators at the Wankdorf Stadium in 1954.

⚓ USA GETS THE BUG ⚓

Despite reputedly being a non-soccer country, USA '94 saw the highest total and average attendances in World Cup history. Some 3.5 million watched the matches at an average of 69,000 per game, compared with 2.5 million and 48,000 in football-mad Italy in 1990.

⚓ TRIBUTE TO AYRTON ⚓

The Brazil team dedicated their World Cup win in 1994 to the memory of racing driver and fellow countryman Ayrton Senna, who had been killed earlier that year in a horrific car crash at the Imola circuit in Italy.

⚓ PATIENCE IS A VIRTUE ⚓

'The World Cup is like a woman. The longer you wait for one, the more you appreciate it.'
– French goalkeeper Lionel Charbonnier gives his opinion on suggestions that the World Cup finals should be held every two years instead of every four

⚓ LOW SCORE ⚓

The 1990 finals in Italy produced the lowest goals-per-game average of any World Cup – just 2.21. It also produced sixteen red cards and 164 yellows at an average of 3.46 cards per match, another unwelcome record.

⚓ LAST AND FIRST ⚓

Alessandro Altobelli of Italy scored the last goal of the 1982 tournament to secure a 3–1 win in the final against West Germany. He also scored the first goal of the 1986 finals, as the defending champions drew 1–1 with Bulgaria.

⚑ HELLO AND GOODBYE ⚑

Argentina's Marcelo Trobbiani made his one and only World Cup appearance as an 88th-minute substitute in the final against West Germany in 1986, equalling the record for the shortest World Cup career set by Tunisia's Khemais Labidi.

⚑ VENUES ⚑

The stadiums selected as venues for the 1966 World Cup in England were:

Manchester (Old Trafford)
Middlesbrough (Ayresome Park)
Sunderland (Roker Park)
Liverpool (Goodison Park)
Sheffield (Hillsborough)
Birmingham (Villa Park)
London (Wembley, White City)

⚑ ENGLAND'S 1966 WORLD CUP-WINNING SQUAD ⚑

Goalkeepers: Gordon Banks, Peter Bonetti, Ron Springett
Defenders: Jimmy Armfield, Gerald Byrne, Jack Charlton, George Cohen, Bobby Moore (c), Ray Wilson
Midfielders: Alan Ball, Ian Callaghan, Bobby Charlton, George Eastham, Ron Flowers, Norman Hunter, Martin Peters, Nobby Stiles
Forwards: John Connelly, Jimmy Greaves, Roger Hunt, Geoff Hurst, Terry Paine
Coach: Alf Ramsey

⚑ GOAL DIFFERENCE ⚑

The 1962 tournament in Chile was the first to apply the goal-difference ruling which would count in the event of two teams being equal on points in the first-round games. In the event, only England needed the new system to progress to the quarter-finals at the expense of Argentina.

⚱ BROKEN LEG TRAGEDY ⚱

The USSR, winner of the inaugural European Nations Cup in 1960, beat Yugoslavia in their first World Cup match in 1962. But what should have been a day of triumph was spoiled when their right-back, Eduard Dubinsky, had his leg badly broken during the match by a vicious tackle by Yugoslav captain Muhamed Mujic. Dubinsky was hospitalised and his career was over, but tragically the injury later caused sarcoma, a form of cancer, which claimed the player's life just a few years later.

⚱ A CUP WITHOUT JULES ⚱

The 1958 World Cup was the first to take place without the familiar figure of the competition's founder, Jules Rimet, who died two years earlier at the age of 83.

⚱ MEMORABLE MORTENSEN ⚱

After boycotting the first three tournaments, England scored their first World Cup goal in the 39th minute of their opening match against Chile at the Maracana Stadium in Rio. The scorer was Stan Mortensen, who latched onto a cross by Jimmy Mullen to head the ball past the curiously named Sergio Livingstone in the Chilean goal.

⚱ BRAZIL NUTS ABOUT THE WORLD CUP ⚱

Thanks largely to the huge crowds, often in excess of 100,000, that packed into the vast bowl of the Maracana Stadium in Rio, the 1950 tournament in Brazil became the first major sporting event to be watched by more than a million spectators.

⚱ OUT AND ABOUT IN ITALY ⚱

Unlike the 1930 World Cup in Uruguay, when all games were played in Montevideo, eight venues were used in Italy four years later: Rome, Naples, Milan, Turin, Florence, Bologna, Genoa and Trieste.

⚱ HOMER SYMPTOM ⚱

No European team has won the World Cup outside of their own continent.

⚲ GREAT GAMES: ROMANIA 3–2 ARGENTINA, 1994 ⚲

Despite losing Maradona to a FIFA ban for drug-taking, Argentina were no pushovers. But then neither were Romania, whose collective will to win allied to the clever prompting of Hagi and Dumitrescu made them the dark horses of the tournament. And despite the best efforts of the reigning World Champions, Romania came good in a fantastic match of swinging fortunes, close shaves and spectacular goals.

⚲ WHERE THE FINALS WERE PLAYED ⚲

Year	Country	City	Stadium	Attendance
1930	Uruguay	Montevideo	Estadio Centenario	93,000
1934	Italy	Rome	Stadio Nazionale	50,000
1938	France	Paris	Stade Colombes	45,124
1950	Brazil	Rio	Maracana	205,000
1954	Switzerland	Berne	Wankdorf Stadium	62,472
1958	Sweden	Stockholm	Rasunda Stadium	49,737
1962	Chile	Santiago	Estadio Nacional	68,679
1966	England	London	Wembley Stadium	93,802
1970	Mexico	Mexico City	Azteca Stadium	107,412
1974	West Germany	Munich	Olympic Stadium	77,833
1978	Argentina	Buenos Aires	Monumental Stadium	76,609
1982	Spain	Madrid	Bernabeu Stadium	90,089
1986	Mexico	Mexico City	Azteca Stadium	114,580
1990	Italy	Rome	Olympic Stadium	73,603
1994	USA	Pasadena	Rose Bowl	94,194
1998	France	Paris	Stade de France	75,000
2002	Japan/S. Korea	Yokohama	Yokohama International	69,029
2006	Germany	Berlin	Olympiastadion	69,000

⚲ FOREIGN FOOD ⚲

On their way to the 1962 World Cup semi-final, the Chilean team claimed their diet was the major reason for success. No doubt in a very early version of media spin, they claimed they ate Swiss cheese to beat the Swiss and spaghetti to beat Italy, and drank vodka to beat USSR. Brazilian coffee clearly didn't agree with them, because they were beaten 4–2 by Garrincha and co.

⚓ A FIRST FOR BERLIN ⚓

The Olympic Stadium in Berlin hosted the 2006 World Cup final. But although the design was all-new, the stadium has a long and chequered history. Here are ten things you should know:

1. The original stadium was built to house the aborted 1916 Olympics.
2. The stadium was rebuilt by Hitler for the 1936 Olympics. After the war, it was used by the British army as their headquarters and remained so until 1994.
3. The 1936 stadium was built by the son of the architect who designed the 1916 version.
4. The stadium is the home ground of Hertha Berlin.
5. It was used for three matches in the 1974 World Cup finals.
6. The stadium was renovated in 2004 after Germany was given the go-ahead to host the 2006 finals.
7. It will host six matches in 2006, including the final.
8. The capacity is 76,000, making it the second largest stadium in Germany behind the Olympic Stadium in Munich.
9. It cost €240 million (£140 million) to renovate.
10. The roof on the stands is a cantilever with a circumference of 840m.

⚓ HOME FROM HOME ⚓

Such is the cosmopolitan nature of English football, it's estimated that nearly 100 foreign players currently plying their trade in the Football League will be included in World Cup squads setting off for South Africa in 2010. Compare this to 1950 when there was just one English-based foreign player, Newcastle's George Robledo, who played for Chile. The foreign legion could include:

Brazil
Lucas, Fabio Aurelio (Liverpool); Heurelho Gomes (Tottenham); Robinho (Manchester City); Anderson (Manchester United); Alex (Chelsea)

Chile
Gonzalo Jara (West Bromwich Albion)

Paraguay
Roque Santa Cruz (Manchester City); Paolo Da Silva (Sunderland)

Argentina
Fabricio Coloccini, Jonas Gutierrez (Newcastle); Javier Mascherano, Maxi Rodriguez (Liverpool); Carlos Tevez (Manchester City)

Uruguay
Diego Arismendi (Stoke City)

USA
Tim Howard, Landon Donovan (Everton); Brad Guzan (Aston Villa); Marcus Hahnemann (Wolves); Jay DeMerit (Watford); Jonathan Spector (West Ham); Clint Dempsey (Fulham); Stuart Holden (Bolton Wanderers); Kenny Cooper (Plymouth Argyle); Jozy Altidore (Hull City)

Mexico
Carlos Vela (Arsenal); Guillermo Franco (West Ham)

Honduras
Wilson Palacios (Tottenham); Osman Chaves (Newcastle); Hendry Thomas (Wigan)

Australia
Mark Schwarzer (Fulham); Brad Jones, Rhys Williams (Middlesbrough); Adam Federici, Oliver Bozanic (Reading); Michael Theoklitos (Norwich); Patrick Kisnorbo (Leeds United); Brett Emerton, Vince Grella (Blackburn Rovers); Tim Cahill (Everton); Dean Heffernan (Huddersfield); Shane Lowry (Aston Villa); Nick Carle (Crystal Palace); Aaron Mooy (Bolton Wanderers); Richard Garcia (Hull City)

New Zealand
Ryan Nelsen (Blackburn Rovers); Chris Killen (Middlesbrough); Chris Wood (West Bromwich Albion); Rory Fallon (Plymouth Argyle); Kris Bright (Shrewsbury Town)

Korea Republic
Park Ji-Sung (Manchester United); Lee Chung-Yong (Bolton Wanderers)

Denmark
Thomas Sorensen (Stoke City); Lars Jacobsen (Blackburn Rovers); Daniel Agger (Liverpool); Nicklas Bendtner (Arsenal)

Germany
Michael Ballack (Chelsea); Robert Huth (Stoke City)
Switzerland
Philippe Senderos (Everton); Johan Djourou (Arsenal); Valon Behrami (West Ham)

Slovakia
Marek Cech (West Bromwich Albion); Martin Skrtel (Liverpool); Vladimir Weiss (Bolton Wanderers); Lubomir Michalik (Leeds United)

Spain
Cesc Fabregas (Arsenal); Pepe Reina, Fernando Torres (Liverpool)

Serbia
Vladimir Stojkovic (Wigan); Nemanja Vidic (Manchester United); Branislav Ivanovic (Chelsea); Nenad Milijas (Wolves)

Italy
Alberto Aquilani (Liverpool)

Netherlands
Robin van Persie (Arsenal); Johnny Heitinga (Everton); Nigel de Jong (Manchester City); Dirk Kuyt, Ryan Babel (Liverpool)

France
Bacary Sagna, William Gallas, Gael Clichy, Mikael Silvestre, Abou Diaby, Samir Nasri (Arsenal); Patrice Evra (Manchester United); Florent Malouda, Nicolas Anelka (Chelsea); Patrick Vieira (Manchester City)

Portugal
Hilario, Ricardo Carvalho, Paolo Ferreira, Jose Bosingwa, Deco (Chelsea); Nani (Man Utd); Luis Boa Morte (West Ham)

Slovenia
Robert Koren (West Bromwich Albion); Suad Filekovic (Barnsley)

Greece
Sotirios Kyrgiakos (Liverpool); Angeloa Basinas (Portsmouth)

South Africa
Benni McCarthy (West Ham); Aaron Mokoena (Portsmouth); Kagiso Dikgacoi (Fulham); Steven Pienaar (Everton)

Ivory Coast
Dider Drogba, Salomon Kalou (Chelsea); Kolo Toure (Manchester City), Abdoulye Meite (West Bromwich Albion); Aruna Dindane (Portsmouth); Steve Gohouri (Wigan)

Ghana
Michael Essien (Chelsea); Richard Kingson (Wigan); John Paintsil (Fulham); John Mensah (Sunderland)

Algeria
Nadir Belhadj (Portsmouth); Hameur Bouazza (Blackpool); Hassan Yebda (Portsmouth); Kamel Ghilas (Hull City)

Cameroon
Alexander Song (Arsenal); Andre Bikey (Burnley); Sebastien Bassong, Benoit Assou-Ekotto (Tottenham)

Nigeria
Aiyegbeni Yakubu, Joseph Yobo, Victor Anichebe (Everton); Danny Shittu (Bolton Wanderers); Mikel John Obi (Chelsea); Seyi Olofinjana (Hull City); Dickson Etuhu (Fulham); Nwankwo Kanu (Portsmouth); Kayode Odejayi (Colchester United); Sam Sodje (Charlton Athletic)

⊥ HOW IT ALL BEGAN ⊥

International football had been around since the late 19th century, and by 1908 the Olympic Games had its own fully fledged tournament (the UK beat Denmark to win gold). By the late 1920s, however, the growth of the game – and in particular professionalism – meant that football was crying out for a competition of its own. FIFA (Fédération Internationale de Football Association) had been formed in 1904 and in 1929, 25 of its 30 member nations voted for a tournament to be held within a year. The architects of the first World Cup were French. The original idea was drafted by FIFA member Henry Delaunay and the final nod of assent to the tournament was given by the president of the organisation, Jules Rimet. If they'd had it their way, the first tournament would have been held in France too – but there was only one member nation willing not only to meet the costs of staging such a global event but to pay the expenses of every country that took part. So it was that in 1930 the first World Cup took place in Uruguay.

⊥ GOLDEN BALLS ⊥

Since 1982 the most outstanding player of the tournament has received the Golden Ball. The winner is voted for by the media from a shortlist drawn up by the FIFA technical committee. The second and third-placed runners-up in this vote are awarded the silver ball and the bronze ball:

1982 Spain:
1. Paolo Rossi (ITA) Goals 6, assists 0, mins played 575
2. Falcao (BRA) Goals 3, assists 0, mins played 450
3. Karl-Heinz Rummenigge (GER) Goals 5, assists 0, mins played 572

1986 Mexico:
1. Diego Maradona (ARG) Goals 5, assists 0, mins played 572
n.b. no silver or bronze balls were officially awarded in 1986, although they were retrospectively awarded to Harald Schumacher (GER) and Preben Elkjær (DEN).

1990 Italy:
1. Salvatore Schillaci (Italy) Goals 6, assists 0, mins played 535
2. Lothar Matthaus (GER) Goals 4, assists 0, mins played 660
3. Diego Maradona (ARG) Goals 0, assists 0, mins played 690

1994 USA:
1. Romario (BRA) Goals 5, assists 0, mins played 660
2. Roberto Baggio (ITA) Goals 5, assists 0, mins played 603
3. Hristo Stoichkov (BUL) Goals 6, assists 0, mins played 644

1998 France:
1. Ronaldo (BRA) Goals 5, assists 0, mins played 660
2. Davor Suker (CRO) Goals 6, assists 0, mins played 630
3. Lilian Thuram (FRA) Goals 2, assists 0, mins played 600

2002 Korea/Japan:
1. Oliver Kahn (GER) Goals 0, assists 0 (GK), mins played 630
2. Ronaldo (BRA) Goals 8, assists 0, mins played 548
3 Hong Myung Bo (KOR) Goals 0, assists 0, mins played 596

2006 Germany:
1. Zinedine Zidane (FRA) Goals 3, assists 1, mins played 559
2. Fabio Cannavaro (ITA) Goals 0, assists 0, mins played 690
3. Andrea Pirlo (ITA) Goals 1, assists 3, mins played 668

⚓ OH NO, GINOLA ⚓

Despite possessing one of the most talented squads in the world, France failed to make the 1994 finals in the USA. The manner of their elimination was painful to behold – and especially for one of the most talented Frenchmen of them all. With the score at 1–1 and needing only to draw against Bulgaria to secure qualification after a ropey passage which had included defeat to Israel, the French were awarded a free-kick deep in opposition territory. There were just 30 seconds of time remaining and already 70,000 fans in the Parc des Princes were thinking about buying plane tickets to the States. Then, disaster. The ball found David Ginola, the long-haired, extravagantly talented left-winger. Instead of playing keep-ball for the remaining seconds, Ginola instead took on his man and lofted a curling cross into the box. The French forwards were not expecting it, and neither were the rest of the team as Bulgaria nabbed possession and broke forward with lightning speed. The ball found Emil Kostadinov, who thrashed it into the back of the net with just ten seconds remaining. France were out of the World Cup and despite his grovelling apology – 'I have no words to describe this moment' – Ginola would never play for his country again.

♁ MARADONA'S FALL FROM GRACE ♁

After lighting up the 1986 and, to a lesser extent the 1990, tournaments, Diego Maradona was hauled back from retirement to bolster a struggling Argentina side in their 1994 campaign in the USA. Despite four turbulent years of cocaine abuse during which he had attacked reporters with an air rifle, Maradona arrived in the US looking leaner and fitter than ever before and it seemed at first that the little man's presence was indeed having a galvanising effect on his team-mates. In their first game against Greece, Argentina were ahead after just 70 seconds and went onto canter home 4–0. Maradona himself scored a wondrous third goal, but this was overshadowed by an extraordinary celebration in which his wide-eyed mask of triumph was thrust directly into the lens of a pitch-side camera. It was not until after the next game, a 2–1 win over Nigeria, that his behaviour was explained. A drugs test revealed a cocktail of five banned drugs in his bloodstream, all belonging to the ephedrine family. Ephedrine, while most commonly found in nasal sprays, is also a stimulant which can aid weight loss. Despite the usual pleas of ignorance, the greatest player of modern times was caught red-handed and immediately kicked out of the tournament and banned from the game. He returned to Argentina in disgrace – ironically needing to have played just one more game to break the record for World Cup appearances.

♁ JACK'S BOYS DO THE BUSINESS ♁

When Ireland played their opening match of the 1994 World Cup at the Giants Stadium in New York, it is estimated that more than 50,000 of the 73,000 capacity crowd were supporting Jack Charlton's men as they defeated Italy 1–0.

♁ SENT-OFF KEEPER ♁U

Although the dubious honour should have, without doubt, gone to West Germany's Harald Schumacher for his assault on Battiston twelve years earlier, the first goalkeeper to be sent off in World Cup finals was Italy's Gianluca Pagliuca for the comparatively mild offence of handling the ball outside his penalty area during a match against Norway in 1994.

♁ EURO QUARTERS ♁

In 1994 all but one of the quarter-finalists were from Europe, the first time since 1958. In both cases the sole South American representative was Brazil – and on both occasions they went on to lift the trophy.

⚱ GORDON BANKS'S SAVE ⚱

In an earlier game against Czechoslovakia in 1970, Pelé had come within inches of scoring a sensational goal when his 60-yard shot just missed the post. Against England, the Brazilian wizard was responsible for forcing what is widely regarded as the competition's most extraordinary save when his bullet header was somehow clawed off the line and over the bar by Gordon Banks. What made the save special was that in order to make it, Banks had to leap from his near post to the far post in a split-second, twisting in mid-air in order to get his outstretched hand to the ball.

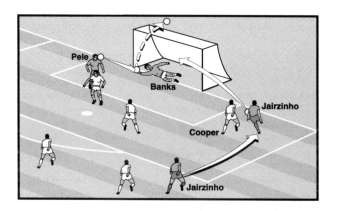

⚱ LANGUAGE BARRIER ⚱

Cameroon were the surprise performers of the 1990 World Cup, beating Argentina, Colombia and Romania before almost defeating England in the quarter-finals. What made their progress even more remarkable was that they were coached by Valeri Nepomniaschi, a Siberian whose only previous managerial experience was in the Soviet second division. Because he spoke no French, Nepomniaschi relied upon a driver from the Soviet embassy in Rome to translate his team talks – and it was widely suspected that the driver, himself a keen amateur player, infused many of the manager's tactics with his own.

⚓ THE HAND OF GOD – AGAIN ⚓

Maradona's personal relationship with the Hand of God made headlines in 1986, and four years later in Italy it seemed the bond was just as strong. Under the cosh against the Soviet Union in their pool match in Bari, the Argentine skipper found himself defending his own goal-line as a header from Kuznetzov arrowed its way towards the net. It would have been a certain goal had the Hand of God not shot out to deflect the ball round the post. In many ways Maradona's hand-ball was even more blatant than the one against England – but, miraculously, referee Erik Frederiksson of Sweden didn't see it. Argentina went on to win 2–0, Maradona went unpunished, and the only sinner was deemed to be Frederiksson who was sent home early accused of incompetence.

⚓ DON'T COUNT OUT COSTA RICA ⚓

During the course of their 1990 qualifying campaign, Costa Rica went through five managers and three FA presidents. It was no surprise, then, that the minnows were rated at a whopping 1,000–1 outsiders to win in Italy. Even less of a surprise that in their first game they beat Scotland by a goal to nil. Managed by Velibor Milutinovic, who had been in charge of hosts Mexico in 1986, they would confound everyone by also beating Sweden and qualifying for the next phase.

⚓ STATUESQUE GOALKEEPER ⚓

Undisputed hero of Costa Rica's epic 1990 World Cup run was goalkeeper Gabelo Conejo, whose acrobatics between the sticks helped propel the 1,000–1 outsiders to the second phase. After the tournament, a statue was erected in Conejo's honour in the Costa Rican capital San José.

⚓ STALLED FERRARI ⚓

As an incentive to qualify for the second phase of the 1990 World Cup, each United Arab Emirates player was promised the reward of a Ferrari Testarossa. Sadly they lost all three pool games, conceding eleven goals. However, striker Khalid Mubarak did bag himself a Rolls-Royce for scoring the UAE's only goal. In 1994 each member of the team received £100,000 and a new Mercedes for qualifying for the finals.

⚓ MANAGEMENT MATERIAL? ⚓

In later years they would both become managers of their respective countries, but as players in 1990, Holland's Frank Rijkaard and Rudi Voller of West Germany provided one of the World Cup's more memorable spats – literally:

- 21 minutes have been played. Rijkaard fouls Voller, who dives outrageously.
- Referee Jana Carlos Loustau of Argentina cautions Rijkaard, which means he will be suspended for the next game.
- Rijkaard spits at Voller, who complains to the referee.
- The referee books Voller.
- Two minutes later Voller and Rijkaard get tangled up in another challenge.
- The referee sends both players off.
- As they leave the pitch, Rijkaard spits at Voller one more time.

⚓ TOO MUCH TO BEAR ⚓

England squeaked past Cameroon to reach the semi-finals of the 1990 World Cup, but it was the Africans who had captured the hearts of the estimated two billion TV viewers watching the tournament across the world. Their departure was too much to bear for one Bangladeshi woman, however, who hanged herself shortly after the final whistle. Her suicide note read: 'The elimination of Cameroon also means the end of my life.'

⚓ NATIONAL FERVOUR ⚓

Before Argentina's 1990 quarter-final against Italy, Diego Maradona – then playing for Napoli – urged all Neapolitans to support the South American side, claiming that for centuries they had been oppressed by the rich north of the country. Needless to say, he was roundly booed from that moment on.

⚓ ZENGA BEATEN ⚓

Claudio Caniggia's goal for Argentina in the 67th minute of their semi-final tie against Italy in 1990 was the first to be conceded by Italian goalkeeper Walter Zenga in 517 minutes of World Cup football Zenga's record eclipsed that of England's Peter Shilton by just eighteen minutes but Italy were defeated in a penalty shoot-out.

⚓ PENALTY ⚓

World Cup 1990 was the first time both semi-finals were decided by penalty shoot-outs.

⚓ NESSUN DORMA ⚓

Pavarotti's version of *Nessun Dorma* became a huge hit when it was used as the theme tune for BBC's coverage of the 1990 World Cup finals in Italy. The Beeb were about to commission their own music when presenter Desmond Lynam suggested the Puccini aria. Its success led to a resurgence in the popularity of opera, and in the career of Pavarotti, who subsequently joined forces to sing it with Plácido Domingo and José Carreras in their globetrotting Three Tenors tours.

⚓ GAZZA'S TEARS ⚓

Paul Gascoigne had been the undisputed star of England's rollercoaster World Cup '90, which began ignominiously but ended with Bobby Robson's men very nearly reaching the final. It was in the semi-final against West Germany that the bubbly Geordie – described by Robson as being 'daft as a brush' – captured the hearts of the world. With the scores tied and the match into extra-time Gazza lunged at Berthold and was booked. The yellow card meant only one thing: if England won, Gascoigne would have to sit out the final. Gazza knew this all too well – and promptly burst into floods of tears. 'Have a word with him,' a concerned Gary Lineker mouthed to the touchline. To his credit, Gazza played on with his customary ebullience as England earned a penalty shoot-out. But although the Germans won through to the final, Gascoigne's global fame and subsequent riches meant that the match had only one winner.

⚓ BRAZIL CHEEK ⚓

Having won the World Cup in 1958 and 1962, Brazil were understandably favourites to complete their hat-trick in England in 1966. Indeed the Brazilians were so confident of winning, and thereby keeping the Jules Rimet trophy in perpetuity, they even offered to replace it with another called the Winston Churchill Cup. In the end, they would have to wait four more years before claiming the Jules Rimet trophy as their own, winning the World Cup in Mexico.

⚓ BERT ON THE MARK ⚓

First player to score a hat-trick in a World Cup match was Bert Patenaude of the USA, who bagged three against Paraguay in the first round of the 1930 World Cup in Uruguay.

⚓ LOTS ⚓

The Republic of Ireland and Holland finished with identical records in Group F of the 1990 World Cup finals in Italy, and with England winning the group, had to draw lots for second and third places. Ireland drew second and went on to face Romania; Holland played West Germany.

⚓ OLD RIVALS ⚓

Sweden have played Brazil seven times in World Cup history. No other countries have met more often.

⚓ WORLD CUP ALL-TIME TOP SCORERS 1930–2009 ⚓

15 Ronaldo (BRA)
14 Gerd Müller (GER)
13 Just Fontaine (FRA)
12 Pelé (BRA)
11 Sandor Kocsis (HUN)
11 Jürgen Klinsmann (GER)
10 Helmut Rahn (GER)
10 Teofilio Cubillas (PER)
10 Gary Lineker (ENG)
10 Grzegorz Lato (POL)
10 Gabriel Batistuta (ARG)
10 Miroslav Klose (GER)
9 Roberto Baggio (ITA)
9 Paolo Rossi (ITA)
9 Uwe Seeler (GER)
9 Jairzinho (BRA)
9 Eusebio (POR)
9 Karl-Heinz Rummenigge (GER)
9 Vava (BRA)
9 Ademir (BRA)
9 Christian Vieri (ITA)

⚓ SUKUR PUNCH ⚓

One of the biggest surprises about Vaclav Masek's goal for
Czechoslovakia after just fifteen seconds of their tie against
Mexico in 1962 is that it should stand for so long as the
quickest in a World Cup. After all, fifteen seconds is quite
a long time when, as Brian Clough once observed, it only
takes a second to score a goal. In fact the record would last
for 40 years. It was finally shattered by Turkey's Hakan
Sukur in the third-place play-off match against co-hosts
South Korea on 28 June 2002. Just eleven seconds were on
the clock when Sukur pounced on a defensive error to
hammer the ball into the back of the net.

⚓ THE ETERNAL NUMBER 12 ⚓

Poland's Leslaw Cmikiewiez played in all six matches of Poland's 1974
World Cup campaign – coming on as substitute each time.

⚓ LAST-GASP PLATT ⚓

England's 1990 World Cup campaign is remembered fondly as the one that got away, thanks to West Germany's unerring accuracy in penalty shoot-outs. But the rose-tinted spectacles hide what was, for the most part, a finals to which Bobby Robson's men were clinging on by their fingernails. Having stuttered through the first round, their second round match against Belgium was just a minute away from penalties when Gerets brought down Gascoigne 40 yards out. Gazza's precise, inswinging free-kick was met by David Platt (a 71st minute substitute for Steve McMahon), who got his foot around the ball and diverted it into the net past Preud'homme. Timed at 119 minutes, it remains the latest goal ever scored in a World Cup tie.

⚓ KISS OF DEATH ⚓

The fastest hat-trick in World Cup history was scored by Hungary's Laszlo Kiss, who scored in the 70th, 74th and 77th minutes against El Salvador in 1982. The feat is somewhat diminished by the fact that the South Americans were already 5–1 down and would go on to lose the match by a record score of 10–1. But then again, Kiss had only been on the field himself for fifteen minutes, having come on as a second-half substitute (he is, in fact, the only substitute to have scored a hat-trick).

⚓ MILLA TIME ⚓

An indication of the longevity of Cameroon's Roger Milla is that his final appearance in a World Cup finals was in 1994 – eighteen years since he first won Africa's footballer of the year award at the age of 24. In the USA Milla was 42 years old and even he would admit he was past his sell-by date. Cameroon, similarly, were but a shadow of the team which had delighted the world by reaching the quarter-finals four years earlier. This time they failed to win a game. However this did not stop Milla appearing twice as a substitute and scoring his customary goal. In fact his close-range toe-poke against Russia in the 47th minute made him not only the oldest player to have scored a goal in a World Cup, but at the time the fastest substitute scorer, having been brought on at half-time.

⚓ PELÉ STATES HIS CASE ⚓

There were those in the Brazilian camp who thought Pelé was too young and irresponsible to play for the team in the 1958 World Cup finals. They soon changed their minds when he produced a sublime performance in his debut in the second round against the USSR. And the youngster reinforced his point in the quarter-final match against Wales with a deflected goal in the 71st minute. Aged just seventeen years and 239 days he remains the youngest player to have scored in a World Cup.

⚓ GOAL A GAME ⚓

The only players to have scored in every World Cup match are Alcide Ghiggia of Uruguay, who managed the feat in 1950, and Jairzinho of Brazil, who did it twenty years later. Of the two, Jairzinho's achievement is the more impressive, as he played in six games whereas Ghiggia scored in every match but Uruguay only played four games.

⚓ SAND OF TIME ⚓

The fastest goal by a substitute was scored by Ebbe Sand of Denmark against Nigeria in the second round in 1998. Sand scored only sixteen seconds after coming on in Denmark's 4–1 win.

⚓ FOUR AN UNLUCKY NUMBER ⚓

On any other day, Polish marksman Ernst Willimowski's feat of scoring four goals in a World Cup match would have grabbed all the headlines and made him a global superstar. Sadly Willimowski's moment of glory came in 1938 against Brazil, who just happened to score six that day to secure a 6–5 victory. The four goals also lose lustre if you consider that Brazil's Leonidas is credited with scoring four himself that day (although some sources claim he only scored three). At least Willimowski earns himself the dubious accolade of being the only man in World Cup history to score four goals and end up on the losing side.

⚓ A GOAL FOR EACH SIDE ⚓

Robert Prosinecki is the only player in World Cup history to have scored for two countries. In 1990, representing Yugoslavia, he bagged a goal against the United Arab Emirates. Eight years later, Yugoslavia was no more and Prosinecki was playing for Croatia when he scored against Jamaica.

⚱ OH NO – OWN GOAL! ⚱

It's the record that nobody wants but somebody has to have – and the honour goes to the unfortunate Ernst Lotscher of Switzerland who in 1938 became the first player to score an own goal in a World Cup match when he put through his own net in a first-round replay against Germany.

⚱ SUBS UP IN MEXICO ⚱

Up until 1970, the use of substitutes was seen as somewhat unmanly. Unless they had a broken leg, players even at the very top level tended to play on. The Mexico tournament, as well as being the first to introduce red and yellow cards, was also the first to feature substitutes. The first was Anatoly Puzach of the USSR who came on at half-time in the opening match against Mexico.

⚱ GREAT GAMES: BELGIUM 4–3 USSR (AET), 1986 ⚱

In the sweltering heat of Leon in Mexico, few expected two European sides to produce such superb entertainment – but Belgium and the USSR conjured a seven-goal thriller in which the only unfortunate aspect was that one of them had to be eliminated from the tournament at the end. Belanov, European footballer of the Year, started the ball rolling with a magnificent strike after 27 minutes – one of three goals for the Soviet star in the match. But in a game of roller-coaster fortunes, rattling woodwork, penalty appeals and two suspicious-looking Belgian goals, the match was decided in extra-time with goals by Demol and Claesen.

⚑ THE HAND OF GOD ⚑

No matter how many brilliant goals Diego Maradona scored in his long World Cup career, the one which stands out more than any other – more even than the magnificent 50-yard solo dribble that followed it – is the so-called 'Hand of God' goal against England in the quarter-final of the 1986 tournament in Mexico. The facts of the matter are these: in the 51st minute Steve Hodge attempted a clearance from the edge of his own penalty area which sliced horrendously across the 18-yard line; Maradona raced in and jumped with Peter Shilton; Maradona punched the ball over Shilton's head into the back of the net; the referee allowed the goal. The Argentine skipper later described his deliberate handball as 'The Hand of God', and for some bizarre reason that excuse seemed to placate the authorities who could have issued Maradona with a one-match ban. Instead, he was vindicated by his second goal four minutes later and by his all-round brilliance in the tournament as a whole. Would England have won if their confidence hadn't been rocked by Maradona's cheating? Probably not. After all, the West Germans failed to recover from Geoff Hurst's debatable second goal in the 1966 final. But in 1986 television technology was twenty years advanced, and it was clear from the very first replay that the goal should not have stood. Maradona and Argentina went on to win the match and the World Cup.

⚑ GOAL IN A THOUSAND ⚑

With Scotland needing to win by three clear goals against Holland to salvage their disastrous 1978 World Cup campaign there was a great deal at stake when Stuart Kennedy upended Johnny Rep to concede a 34th minute penalty. Certainly no-one in the San Martin stadium in Mendoza was aware that if Robbie Rensenbrink converted the spot-kick he would be reaching a World Cup milestone, least of all Rensenbrink himself. The Dutchman duly scored and thereby notched the 1,000th goal in World Cup history.

⚭ GOLDEN GOAL ⚭

Ever since it was invented, football mandarins have been trying to get rid of the dreaded penalty shoot-out as a means of deciding stalemate matches. In 1996 FIFA introduced the so-called 'Golden Goal' in the European Championships in England. It meant that if a match went into extra-time, the first team to score would immediately win the match. On paper it seemed like a good idea – but when a Golden Goal decided the final between Germany and the Czech Republic, fans were left feeling even more cheated than if the match had been decided on penalties. The system was used for the first time in the World Cup two years later, and, fittingly, it was France who benefited when Laurent Blanc's extra-time strike secured a 1–0 win over Paraguay. In 2003, the Golden Goal became the Silver Goal – this time the team leading after the first fifteen-minute period of extra-time would win. Thankfully in 2004 the whole system was scrapped. It seemed that, however unsatisfactory, penalties were here to stay.

⚭ SWEATING IN MOTOWN ⚭

In a bid to add some razzmatazz to the 1994 World Cup, the Americans decreed that the match between the hosts and Switzerland would be played, for the first time, indoors. The venue was the Pontiac Silverdome in Detroit. Usually the home of the Detroit Lions grid-iron team, the stadium is perfect for those freezing Midwest nights during the NFL season. But in the height of a roasting summer, and with 73,000 fans packed to the rafters, the effect was to slowly boil the players of both sides and coat the grass with a veneer of moisture. It was not long before the teams were reduced to walking pace, and those who tried to run found themselves slipping on the greasy surface. The match finished 1–1, which in itself was an effort worthy of congratulation.

⚐ NORTH KOREA MAGIC ⚐

For the people of Middlesbrough, the North Korean side of 1966 must have seemed impossibly exotic – if not a little frightening. But it did not take long for the men from South East Asia to win the hearts of the Teessiders, with a series of tenacious displays culminating in one of the greatest upsets in World Cup history. Playing with plenty of enthusiasm but little guile, the North Koreans were hammered 3–0 in their first match against the Soviet Union. In their next match, however, they gave an indication of things to come by playing out a spirited 1–1 draw with Chile. Their final group game was against the mighty Italians, who had struggled to beat Chile and gone down 1–0 to the Soviets. Nevertheless, they were expected to crush the North Koreans and thereby qualify for the next round. Fielding seven changes, Italy set about the minnows with gusto. But brave defending kept the scores level, and then things gradually began to fall apart for Fabri, the Italian manager. First Bulgarelli departed with a knee injury after 35 minutes. Then, with just three minutes to go to half-time, a sweeping North Korean move ended with Pak Doo-ik scoring with a spectacular strike. Stunned, the Italians were unable to rouse themselves in the second half and, to the delight of the underdog-supporting Englishmen packed into Ayresome Park, North Korea ran out winners. Things got even worse for the Italians who, having been ignominiously eliminated, returned to a barrage of rotten fruit and vegetables at Rome airport.

⚐ NORTH KOREA AGAIN ⚐

Having stunned the footballing world by beating Italy in the group stages of the 1966 finals, North Korea seemed destined to create an even bigger surprise in the quarter-final tie against Eusebio's Portuguese. Having taken a shock lead in the first minute at Goodison Park, the North Koreans promptly doubled it, then scored a third to lead 3–0 with barely 25 minutes gone.

With his dream of World Cup glory slipping fast, it was Eusebio himself who took a decisive grip on proceedings. First, he scored a magnificent solo goal to bring Portugal back into the match then, just before half-time, he converted a penalty after Torres was brought crashing down in the box. In the second half, Eusebio was untouchable, scoring two more goals – including a second penalty – and setting up a fifth to send Portugal through to a semi-final clash with England.

The day, however, belonged to the gallant North Koreans who, having already won an army of supporters in Middlesbrough, now counted the people of Liverpool among their most fervent admirers.

⚓ NORTH KOREA DISAPPOINT ⚓

They were the stars of the 1966 World Cup but, four years later North Korea were absent from the finals in Mexico. Indeed they were unceremoniously booted out of the qualifying rounds by FIFA after refusing to play Israel.

⚓ RECORD ATTENDANCE ⚓

The game between Brazil and Paraguay at the Maracana Stadium on 31 August 1969 attracted 183,341 spectators – a record for a World Cup qualifying game.

⚓ A PUZZLING DECISION ⚓

There have been many head-scratching decisions by World Cup referees, but perhaps none as baffling – or as suspicious – as that by Egypt's Ali Kandil during a group game between Mexico and El Salvador in 1970. Having awarded a free-kick to El Salvador, Kandil then proceeded to watch as Mexico's Padilla took the kick and found his team-mate Valdivia who promptly scored. Despite the understandable protests of the El Salvadorians, Kandil refused to change his mind. Demoralised at what they perceived as blatant favouritism towards the hosts, El Salvador collapsed in the second half and lost 4–0.

⚓ MEXICO HELPED OUT AGAIN? ⚓

Having already benefited from a highly dubious refereeing decision in their 1970 group game against El Salvador, hosts Mexico continued to enjoy the largesse of the man in black in their next game against Belgium. Striker Valdivia seemed the only one to blame when, running into the Belgian penalty area, he tripped and fell over the prostrate Jeck, who had been laid out in a previous challenge. Unbelievably, the Argentinian referee awarded the spot-kick, which Pena gleefully converted to give Mexico a 1–0 and winning lead.

⚱ BOBBY AND THE BRACELET ⚱

It seemed barely credible, but in May 1970, on a stop-over in Colombia en route to the 1970 finals in Mexico, England's upstanding captain Booby Moore found himself under arrest for the suspected theft of an emerald bracelet from a local shop. Despite international protests, Moore was detained under house arrest in Bogotá while the legal teams of both countries got to work. The case itself was a travesty: the chief witness to the alleged crime turned out to be the owner of a jewellery shop and not a passer-by as he first stated; Moore's chief accuser, shop assistant Clara Padilla, fled to the USA before she could be cross-examined; and the shop owner Danilo Rojas claimed £6,000 damages for a bracelet which cost £600. Indeed the whole scam was something which tourists regularly found themselves falling victim to.

Typically phlegmatic, Moore organised practice kick-arounds involving himself, the guards and the local children. This made him immensely popular with the Colombians who pressured for his release. After four days under arrest, he was allowed to rejoin the rest of the squad in Mexico before the charges were eventually dropped. The case wasn't officially closed for five years, during which time Moore said that whenever he walked into a jewellery shop 'I have to keep my hands behind my back and point with my nose'.

⚱ PELÉ MAKES A POINT ⚱

Having been rough-housed out of the 1966 finals, Pelé had threatened to boycott the 1970 finals in Mexico – indeed he had even threatened to retire altogether. Fortunately, he changed his mind and, at the age of 29, became the fulcrum of one of the finest teams ever to play in the World Cup. It did not take long for the master to make his point: in the first group game against Czechoslovakia, Pelé saw the goalkeeper Viktor off his line and, from all of 60 yards, lazily lobbed it over his head. Fortunately for Viktor, the ball missed the post by inches.

⚓ THE SAVE OF THE CENTURY ⚓

Gordon Banks, commenting on his magnificent save from Pelé in the classic 1970 group match in Guadalajara:

'I moved off my line and as I turned my head I saw Pelé. He met the ball with the meat of his head. Textbook stuff. I heard him shout, "Golo!" I found myself at a 40-degree angle with my right hand stretching out towards the post, my eyes trained in front of me. I knew if I made contact, I'd have to get it up in the air. The ball hit the deck two yards in front of me. I made contact with one finger and rolled my hand, using the third and fourth fingers as leverage. I landed crumpled against the netting and my first reaction was to look at Pelé. He'd ground to a halt. I knew all I needed to know.'

'He came from nowhere,' said Pelé. 'I headed it perfectly towards one corner of the net while Banks was at the other corner. I was already shouting "GOOOL!!!" when Banks, like a salmon leaping up a falls, threw himself in the air and managed to tip the ball over the crossbar. It was an impossible play.'

Pelé: 'I thought that was a goal.'

Banks: 'You and me both.'

Bobby Moore: 'You're getting old, Banksy. You used to hold on to them.'

Banks (to himself): 'Like hell I did.'

⚓ SNIFFER'S BIG DAY ⚓

11 June 1970 was a day to remember for Leeds' Allan Clarke. Not only was it his birthday and his wedding anniversary, but he made his England debut in the group match against Czechoslovakia and scored the winner from the penalty spot.

⚓ RAISING THE CROWD ⚓

Keen to promote the 1970 tournament as the best ever, the Mexican football authorities routinely added thousands to the official attendances of even the most mundane matches.

	Official Attendance	Real Attendance
Belgium vs El Salvador	92,205	30,000
USSR vs El Salvador	89,970	25,000
England vs Czechoslovakia	49,292	35,000
Peru vs Morocco	13,537	7,000
Bulgaria vs Morocco	12,299	400
Uruguay vs USSR	96,085	45,000
West Germany vs Uruguay	104,403	32,000

⚓ POLITICAL DEFEAT ⚓

Labour Prime Minister Harold Wilson blamed England's shock 3–2 quarter-final defeat against West Germany in 1970 for his own defeat in the General Election that year. Prior to the match, the Labour party were seven points ahead in the polls. But four days later Ted Heath swept to power in the second shock result of the week.

⚓ UNLUCKY BELGIUM ⚓

During their qualifying campaign for the 1974 World Cup, Belgium beat Iceland 4–0 home and away, Norway 2–0 home and away, and drew 0–0 with Johan Cruyff's Holland in Antwerp. The return fixture against the Dutch was to be held in Amsterdam, and with both sides on nine points a win for either side would see them qualify at the other's expense. In the event of a draw, goal difference would decide the issue. The match finished 0–0, which meant that the Dutch, having scored more goals against Norway and Iceland, went through. Unbeaten Belgium, despite scoring 12 goals and conceding 0, were nevertheless eliminated.

⚓ ELIMINATED ⚓

So much for the form book; four of the eight quarter-finalists in the 1966 tournament – Portugal, Hungary, North Korea and Argentina – failed to qualify for the finals in Mexico in 1970.

⚐ TWO YELLOWS DOES NOT NECESSARILY EQUAL A RED ⚐

The game between Australia and Chile in Berlin in 1974 was a dire 0–0 draw played by two poor sides who had no hope of progressing beyond the first round. Yet thanks to the differing approach of two referees, the match finds itself – perhaps undeservingly – in the history books. After 37 minutes, Iranian referee Jafar Namdar booked Australia's Ray Richards. Later on in the game, when Richards committed another foul, everyone in the Olympic stadium expected him to be sent off. Instead, whether by accident or design, Namdar brandished another yellow card and allowed him to play on. This outrageous bending of the rules proved too much for reserve referee Clive Thomas of Wales. Thomas, a man who once booked Coventry City's Roy Barry even as he was being stretchered off the pitch with a broken leg, ran down from the stands and informed the linesman of the situation. Namdar was alerted, and Richards was duly sent off – five minutes after receiving his second yellow.

A similarly infamous incident occurred at the 2006 World Cup, during the Group F Croatia vs. Australia match on 22 June. After already sending off two players, Poll failed to send off Croatian defender Josip Šimunic for a second yellow card late in the match (despite vociferous protests from the Australian players), eventually sending him off for a third yellow for dissent at the final whistle. The match ended 2-2, and australia progressed to the next round, but FIFA chief Sepp Blatter later commented that 'had Australia lost the game and gone out of the World Cup, they would have had grounds to request a replay'. Unsurprisingly, Poll was one of the 14 officials dismissed by FIFA from the remaining World Cup matches, and, suitably embarrassed, he boarded the plane home, his international refereeing career effectively over.

⚐ NO OTHER MOTIVATION REQUIRED ⚐

'I didn't give a damn as long as we could humiliate them. They murdered my father, sister and two brothers. I am full of angst. I hate them.'
– Dutch midfielder Willem van Hanegem describing why he did not need motivating for the 1974 World Cup final against West Germany

⚓ LIP FROM DER KAISER ⚓

'You *are* an Englishman, of course!'
– West German skipper Franz Beckenbauer to referee Jack Taylor after he had just awarded Holland a second-minute penalty in the 1974 World Cup final.

⚓ FAME AT LAST ⚓

'Old ladies who had been coming into my shop for years suddenly started talking to me about sweepers and creating space. That's the power of television.'
– Jack Taylor, World Cup referee and Wolverhampton butcher, reflects on the fame he received after the 1974 final

⚓ A SECOND YELLOW FOR CRUYFF ⚓

With his side trailing 2–1 at half-time in the 1974 World Cup final, Dutch captain Johan Cruyff left the pitch moaning about some of the industrial-strength tackling he had been subjected to by the West Germans. His complaining earned him a yellow card from English referee Jack Taylor. In 1999, 25 years after the match, Cruyff and Taylor met again. This time the venue was Barcelona where Cruyff was due to present Taylor with an award signifying his admittance to the FIFA International Hall of Fame. As he approached the stage, Taylor reached into his pocket and produced a yellow card, which he waved at Cruyff. Needless to say, the great Dutchman – and everyone else in the auditorium – saw the funny side.

⚓ IT'S A DOG'S LIFE FOR ALLY ⚓

With his world crumbling around him following a 3–1 defeat against Peru and a dismal 1–1 draw with Iran in the 1978 finals, Scotland boss Ally MacLeod was in reflective mood as he entertained the press at the team's hotel in Cordoba. 'I've few friends left now,' he informed the assembled hacks. At that moment a stray mongrel dog emerged from the undergrowth and trotted up to MacLeod. 'In fact the only friend I have is this wee brown dog,' MacLeod said, reaching down to stroke the animal – who promptly sank his fangs into the Scottish manager's thumb.

⚓ ODE TO ARCHIE ⚓

'It's nae o Argentina that I mind,
Or Brazil, passin their triangles neat.
Na, it's o Archie Gemmill's feet streekin
A pattern on the edge o the box.
His skeely needle threaded the ba past
Three men, their legs fooled by the phantom darner.
It was a baldy-heeded goblin scored the goal.
His shot, a rainbow, arches ower his name.'

– Scottish poet Alastair Mackie waxes lyrical over Archie Gemmill's wonder goal for Scotland against Holland in 1978

⚓ SMOKERS ⚓

Gerson, Brazil's influential midfielder in the 1970 World Cup, smoked three packets of cigarettes a day. Socrates, captain in 1982 and 1986, was a forty-a-day man, as was Osvaldo Ardiles of Argentina in 1978.

⚓ WORST KEEPER ⚓

Tubilandu Dimbi, Zaire's reserve goalkeeper, came on as a substitute 21 minutes into his side's 1974 group game against Yugoslavia. Zaire were already trailing 3–0, and the unfortunate Tubilandu went on to concede a further seven as the Yugoslavs ran riot 9–0. Not only were those torrid 69 minutes the only action Tubilandu saw in the tournament, but statistically those seven goals make him the worst World Cup goalkeeper of all time. Harsh, perhaps – but statistics do not lie.

⚓ SEND IN THE CLOWN ⚓

Poland's goalkeeper Jan Tomaszewski was famously dismissed as a 'clown' by Brian Clough prior to a heroic performance at Wembley which resulted in England failing to qualify for the 1974 World Cup finals in West Germany. Any remaining doubts about his talent were swiftly dismissed in the finals themselves, as Tomaszewski made two penalty saves out of three in the second group stage which helped propel his side as far as the third-place play-off. Here Tomaszewski kept a clean sheet against Brazil as the Poles won 1–0.

⚑ ITALIAN VERDICT ⚑

'The worst England team I have ever seen. Disorganised, confused, of only limited ability.'
– Italian captain Giacinto Facchetti's damning verdict of Don Revie's side, which contained the likes of Keegan, Channon, Brooking, Bowles and Hughes, but which failed to qualify for the 1978 World Cup finals – the second successive failure for England. Facchetti was speaking after Italy had beaten England 2-0 in Rome

⚑ SUPER TUNISIA ⚑

Tunisia's stunning 3–1 win over Mexico in their Group 2 match of the 1978 World Cup earned them the accolade of being the first African nation to win a match at the finals. 'The world has laughed at Africa,' said manager Abdelmajid Chetali, 'but now the mockery is over.'

⚑ DUTCH DISBELIEF ⚑

'You are pulling my trousers!'
– the reaction of a Dutch journalist after being told that Kenny Burns of Scotland's doomed 1978 World Cup squad had just been voted Player of the Year in England

⚑ GREAT GOALS ⚑

In 2000, visitors to the Planet World Cup website were asked to vote for the greatest World Cup goal. Here is their Top Ten:

Diego Maradona, Argentina vs England, 1986
Having benefited from the 'Hand of God' to put Argentina ahead against England, Maradona then proved that he was truly blessed from above with a sensational second. Collecting the ball in the centre circle, the Argentine skipper turned on a sixpence and set off on a run straight at the England defence, leaving Peter Reid, Terry Fenwick and Terry Butcher bamboozled before clipping the ball insolently past Peter Shilton.

Saeed Owairan, Saudi Arabia vs Belgium, 1994
Owairan was known as the Maradona of the Arabs, and he showed why with a quite stunning, mazy run from the edge of his own penalty area that culminated in a thunderous strike for goal. In the past, Saudi players had been offered Rolls-Royces and Ferraris for World Cup success – so we can only guess what gifts were showered on Owairan after this brilliant solo goal.

Arie Haan's thunderbolt vs West Germany 1978

Arie Haan's thunderbolt vs Italy 1978

Arie Haan, Holland vs Italy, 1978

There seemed little danger when Holland midfielder Arie Haan took possession from a free-kick just inside the Italian half. But earlier in the competition Haan had blasted a 30-yard thunderbolt which left West Germany's Sepp Maier helpless and now the Dutchman hit a scarcely credible shot from 40 yards which flew in off a post, leaving veteran keeper Dino Zoff scratching his head.

Pelé, Brazil vs Sweden, 1958
The 17-year-old announced his presence on the world stage with a world-class goal in the 1958 final. As the cross came in from the left, he controlled the ball instantly on his knee, then flipped it nonchalantly over the defender's head before driving it into the back of the net.

Roberto Baggio, Italy vs Czechoslovakia, 1990
Pure genius from Baggio, who ran all the way from half-way line, leaving the Czech defenders in his wake, before planting the ball in the back of the net.

Dennis Bergkamp, Holland vs Argentina, 1998
Sublime artistry from Bergkamp as he controlled de Boer's 50-yard pass with his right foot, stepped away from the Argentine defender, and then curled it with precision into the far corner of the net with his left.

Diego Maradona, Argentina vs Belgium, 1986
There is no such thing as a one-man team, but in 1986 it seemed that Maradona was running the entire World Cup to his own agenda. This goal, although not quite as good as his second against England, was still breathtaking. Again, the little man seemed to thrive on running directly at defenders, beating them and then scoring. Here he took on four Belgians before choosing the perfect moment to clip the ball past the advancing Pfaff.

Gemmill

Archie Gemmill, Scotland vs Holland, 1978

Scotland saved the best till last in their woeful 1978 campaign. Gemmill picked up a loose ball on the right of the Dutch penalty area, came inside Jansen's lunge, beat Krol on the outside, nutmegged Poortvliet then delicately chipped it over the advancing keeper. A brilliant goal, but sadly too little too late for Ally MacLeod's men.

Carlos Alberto, Brazil vs Italy, 1970

Already leading 3–1 in the final, this was the icing on the cake for the brilliant Brazilians. After tricky footwork by Clodoaldo, the ball finally reached Pelé on the edge of the box. His perfect lay-off found the skipper steaming up the right-hand channel, and his thunderous shot was unstoppable.

Manuel Negrete, Mexico vs Bulgaria, 1986

Controlling a difficult bouncing ball with ease on the edge of the area, Negrete played a neat one–two before bursting the net with a stunning mid-air scissor kick from the edge of the box.

⚓ GOLDEN SALENKO ⚓

Few people had even heard of Russia's Oleg Salenko before the 1994 World Cup, let alone expected him to be joint winner of the Golden Boot award for top goal scorer. He ended up with six, alongside Bulgaria's Hristo Stoichkov – thanks largely to scoring five against Cameroon. Had the Russians not been eliminated, he may well have gone on to become the first player for twenty years to score more than six goals in a World Cup tournament.

⚱ GOLDEN BOOTS ⚱

The scorer of the most goals in a tournament is awarded the coveted Golden Boot. The winners since 1930 have been:

1930: Guilermo Stabile (ARG), 8
1934: Oldrich Nejedly (CZE), Angelo Schiavo (ITA); Edmund Conen (GER), 4
1938: Leonidas (BRA), 8
1950: Ademir (BRA), 9
1954: Sandor Kocsis (HUN), 11
1958: Juste Fontaine (FRA), 13
1962: Garrincha (BRA), Valentin Ivanov (SOV), Leonel Sanchez (CHI), Florian Albert (HUN), Vava (BRA), Drazan Jerkovic (YUG), 4
1966: Eusebio (POR), 9
1970: Gerd Muller (GER), 10
1974: Gzegorz Lato (POL), 7
1978: Mario Kempes (ARG), 6
1982: Paolo Rossi (ITA), 6
1986: Gary Lineker (ENG), 6
1990: Salvatore Schillaci (ITA), 6
1994: Hristo Stoichkov (BUL), Oleg Salenko (RUS), 6
1998: Davor Suker (CRO), 6
2002: Ronaldo (BRA), 8
2006: Miroslav Klose (GER), 5

⚱ MOST GOALS IN ONE MATCH ⚱

5 – Oleg Salenko (RUS) vs Cameroon, 1994
4 – Emilio Butragueno (SPA) vs Denmark, 1986
4 – Eusebio (POR) vs North Korea, 1966
4 – Juste Fontaine (FRA) vs West Germany, 1958
4 – Sandor Kocsis (HUN) vs West Germany, 1954
4 – Ademir (BRA) vs Sweden, 1950
4 – Juan Schiaffino (URU) vs Bolivia, 1950
4 – Leonidas (BRA) vs Poland, 1938
4 – Ernst Willimowski (POL) vs Brazil, 1938
4 – Gustav Wetterstrom (SWE) vs Cuba, 1938

⚓ LANDMARK GOALS ⚓

1st – Lucien Laurent (FRA) v Mexico, 1930
500th – Bobby Collins (SCO) v Paraguay, 1958
1000th – Robbie Rensenbrink (HOL) v Scotland, 1978
1500th – Claudio Caniggia (ARG) v Nigeria, 1994
2063rd – Marco Materazzi (ITA) v France, 2006

⚓ TOP TEN SHOCKING RESULTS ⚓

England 0–1 USA, 1950
Billy Wright and co. were humiliated by American part-timers.

North Korea 1–0 Italy, 1966
Fans pelted the *Azzurri* with rotten tomatoes after this horror show at Ayresome Park.

Algeria 2–1 West Germany, 1986
The 1,000–1 outsiders beat the 3–1 favourites. 'I still can't believe this,' said German boss Jupp Derwall. 'It is beyond my understanding.'

Cameroon 1–0 Argentina, 1990
Nine-man Cameroon ran Diego Maradona's men ragged.

Senegal 1–0 France, 2002
The reigning World Champions humbled by minnows making their first appearance in the tournament.

East Germany 1–0 West Germany, 1974
The first meeting between the two teams, and a major upset.

Spain 5–1 Denmark, 1986
Denmark had cruised through the group and were leading this match before a dramatic and inexplicable collapse.

Bulgaria 2–1 Germany, 1994
Germany are leading 1-0 and heading for the semi-finals when Stoitchkov and Letchkov pounce with two goals in two minutes.

Northern Ireland 1–0 Spain, 1982
The hosts are silenced by Gerry Armstrong's emphatic winner.

Cuba 2–1 Romania, 1938
Romania were among the European elite; Cuba had only stepped in at the last minute when Mexico dropped out. The football world was rocked.

⚲ MOROCCO MAGIC ⚲

In reaching the 1970 finals in Mexico, Morocco became the first African side to qualify since Egypt in 1934. And as 500–1 outsiders, they surely deserved more assistance than they received from Dutch referee Laurens van Ravens during their group game with West Germany. Leading a goal to nil, and playing an energetic style of football which had the supposedly superior Europeans rattled, Morocco took to the field for the second half with just ten men while goalkeeper Allal Ben Kassu received some last-minute instructions in the tunnel. To their horror, referee van Ravens blew for the restart and, despite Moroccan protests, let the game continue for over a minute before allowing Kassu back onto the pitch. It was testament to how badly the Germans were playing that they failed to even get a shot in during that time – and that they were relieved to finally run out 2–1 winners.

⚲ BECKENBAUER'S SHOULDER ⚲

West Germany's inspirational Franz Beckenbauer played for more than an hour of his side's epic 1970 semi-final against Italy with a dislocated shoulder.

⚲ HOME ADVANTAGE ⚲

Uruguay complained that Brazil would have home advantage in their World Cup semi-final in 1970 – even though the match was played in Guadalajara, Mexico!

⚲ CUP HOLDERS ⚲

If it were needed, there was an extra spice to the 1970 World Cup final between Italy and Brazil in Mexico. As both teams had won the tournament twice, the winner this time would be allowed to keep the trophy in perpetuity. Brazil, of course, won 4–1.

⚱ OPEN GOAL ⚱

Chile were favourites to qualify for the 1974 World Cup finals in Germany after travelling to Moscow and securing a 0–0 draw in the first leg of their tie against the Soviet Union. And their progress was put beyond all doubt when the Soviets refused to play the second leg. The match was due to be played at the National Stadium in Santiago, but the Soviets complained that the stadium had been used to house thousands of political prisoners when the Chilean military overthrew the Marxist government of President Salvador Allende. Unconcerned with this, FIFA ordered that the match should go ahead. Chile duly kicked off and scored in the empty Soviet net to secure the easiest win in World Cup history.

⚱ MARXIST MARKSMAN ⚱

During their opening game of the 1974 World Cup against the hosts West Germany, the Chile team found itself the target of barracking from a section of Marxist sympathisers in the crowd. The protesters were complaining about the right-wing military coup which had resulted in the overthrow of the democratically elected Marxist government of Salvador Allende. It must have been particularly satisfying, therefore, that the winning goal was scored by Germany's Paul Breitner – himself an avowed Marxist.

⚱ EAST US WEST ⚱

The historic first clash between East and West Germany took place at Hamburg's Volkspark Stadium in 1974. The match was a 60,000 sell-out – although only 3,000 of that number had been granted permission to cross the border following strict security vetting. It was they who had the last laugh, however, as the East ran out 1–0 victors thanks to a late goal by Sparwasser.

⚱ ZAIRE SPIT THE DUMMY ⚱

After losing 9–0 and having a man sent off against Yugoslavia, Zaire were so disheartened they decided to go home from the 1974 World Cup in Germany. Only some frantic behind-the-scenes negotiation by FIFA officials persuaded them to stay. They did – only to lose 3–0 to Brazil.

⚑ HAITI DOPE ⚑

Having taken a shock lead against Italy during a group match in 1974, the minnows of Haiti won widespread praise by only losing by 3–1. However, the Haitian 'management' showed little goodwill when one of their players, Ernst Jean-Joseph, became the first player in World Cup history to be tested positive for drugs. The unfortunate Joseph was sent home in disgrace – having first been dragged from the team's base and beaten up by hired thugs loyal to the dictator 'Papa Doc' Duvalier.

⚑ *WO IST DIE* CORNER FLAGS? ⚑

Before an assembled crowd of 77,833 at Munich's Olympic Stadium, and an estimated worldwide television audience of one billion, Jack Taylor, the English referee, was about to start the 1974 World Cup final between West Germany and Holland – when he noticed the corner flags were missing!

⚑ THE ONE-MINUTE PENALTY ⚑

Holland took the lead in the 1974 World Cup final against West Germany with a penalty by Johan Neeskens after just one minute. In that time the Dutch had kicked off and completed a movement of sixteen passes before Cruyff was brought down in the penalty box. Not one German player had touched the ball.

⚑ NO KIDNAPPINGS TODAY ⚑

Argentina were awarded the 1978 World Cup finals as far back as 1966, when the country was seen as a model of peaceful democracy. Twelve years later, it was run by a brutal military junta and riven with violent insurrection by left-wing terrorists. It was only when the revolutionaries agreed to suspend their programme of killings and kidnappings because 'football is a game of the working class' that FIFA agreed to let the tournament commence.

⚑ GRASS KILLER ⚑

With just weeks to go before the 1978 World Cup in Argentina, a groundsman at the River Plate stadium in Buenos Aires decided to sprinkle the pitch with sea-water. Not surprisingly, the grass promptly died, resulting in the whole pitch having to be returfed.

⚑ HEFTY BILL FOR THE JUNTA ⚑

The right-wing Argentinian junta were so determined to make the 1978 World Cup a showpiece, they spent an estimated £500 million ($700 million) on building stadiums and making existing grounds fit for the tournament. The expenditure also included hiring a public relations firm, razing slums and moving the poor to areas where they wouldn't be visible to the thousands of foreign media and visitors.

⚑ HOME BIAS ⚑

'The host nation always does well traditionally. Everything is in their favour. Even the referees are under the influence of the home crowd.'
– Hungary manager Lajos Baroti, shortly before the opening game of the 1978 World Cup against Argentina. Two of his players were sent off as the host nation won 2–1

⚑ CHANGE STRIPS ⚑

Aware that in 1978 many of the estimated one billion television viewers would be watching on black and white sets, FIFA ordered France (blue) and Hungary (red) to play their group match in change strips. Unfortunately, both teams turned up in all-white kit – resulting in an embarrassing 40-minute delay before a replacement set could be found and the match could kick off.

⚑ RARE GOAL ⚑

Erwin Vandenbergh's winning goal for Belgium against Argentina in the 1982 finals in Spain was the first to be scored in an inaugural match since 1962. It was also the first time the defending champions had lost their opening match since Italy in 1950.

⚥ REFEREEING DECISION ⚥

Sweden and Brazil were playing out a largely uninspiring 1–1 draw in their opening group match of the 1978 finals in Argentina when, in the dying seconds, the Brazilians won a corner. The ball was flighted in by Nelinho and forcefully headed home by Zico – but the Brazilian celebrations were short-lived. In one of the more controversial – not to say pedantic – decisions in World Cup history, Welsh referee Clive Thomas had blown for full-time the moment Nelinho had struck the dead ball.

⚥ DOPE TEST ⚥

It seemed like adding insult to injury when, having been on the end of a humiliating defeat to Peru in the first game of the 1978 World Cup campaign, Scotland's Willie Johnston was drug-tested and found positive for the stimulant fencamfamin. The news provoked one Scottish journalist to remark that Johnston's display in the match was 'so utterly lethargic that one has to seriously question the efficacy of the drug.' Johnston was sent home, protesting that drug taking was standard practice at his club, West Bromwich Albion. His comments led to a major investigation by the Football League, and the introduction of random dope-testing for English clubs.

⚥ OWN GOALS ⚥

'Where are we going to find three Dutchmen to score own goals?'
– Scottish supporter on hearing that in order to qualify for the next stage of the 1978 World Cup finals, his side had to beat Holland by three clear goals. In the event, the Scots won 3–2

⚥ HUNGARY FOR GOALS ⚥

It is one of the great perversities of the World Cup that Hungary failed to win the 1954 tournament, despite scoring a record 27 goals in just five matches, including nine against South Korea, eight against West Germany, and four apiece against Brazil and Uruguay.

⚖ FIX? ⚖

As hosts of the 1978 tournament, Argentina had played well but still found themselves needing to beat Peru by four clear goals to reach the final ahead of arch rivals Brazil. On paper, it seemed an impossible task – but to everyone's astonishment Argentina went on to score six against a strong side who had not conceded more than three goals in any match in the tournament to that point. Surprise quickly turned to suspicion when it was revealed that Admiral Carlos Lacoste, a high-ranking member of the Argentine junta who had served as World Cup organiser and Vice-President of FIFA, had subsequently arranged for 35,000 tons of free grain to be transported to Peru, and that the Argentine Central Bank had unfrozen around $50 million in credits to the Peruvian government. Although Peru's Argentine-born goalkeeper Carlos Quiroga published an open letter defending himself and his team, it did not dispel the notion that the hosts had reached the final courtesy of one of the most outrageous match-fixes of all time.

⚖ PLASTER CAST ⚖

The 1978 World Cup final between Argentina and Holland was billed as a spectacular clash of the best South America and Europe could offer. But no sooner had the ticker-tape been thrown from the towering stands of the River Plate stadium than the match was plunged into controversy. First, the Dutch were left waiting on the pitch for five minutes before the hosts arrived. Then the Argentinians took exception to a small plaster cast which Holland's Rene van der Kerkhof was wearing on his forearm, the result of an injury sustained in the first match. When the Italian referee, Sergio Gonella, upheld the protest, the Dutch threatened to walk off the pitch. (Gonella himself was only selected as referee because the Argentinians had objected to the first choice, an Israeli who, they claimed, had links to the Dutch side.) A compromise was eventually reached when van der Kerkhof agreed to play with a soft covering on his cast, but Holland were rattled and went on to lose their second successive World Cup final 3–1 in extra-time.

⚓ DRAW FARCE ⚓

Spain spent in excess of £60 million on staging the 1982 World Cup. It's just a pity a few quid couldn't have been spent on ensuring the draw for the finals ran smoothly. Watched by an incredulous global TV audience, the list of cock-ups included:

- England were one of the six top seeds, despite the fact they had finished second in their qualifying group and struggled to reach the finals.
- To prevent Peru and Chile from appearing in the same group as South American rivals Brazil and Argentina, the miniature footballs containing their names were supposed to be left out of the metal cage used to make the draw. Somebody forgot to leave them out.
- Scotland were drawn in Argentina's group before it was realised it should have been Belgium. The Scots were drawn again, this time in Brazil's group.
- The metal cage jammed, snapping one of the miniature footballs in half.

⚓ ROSSI'S TRIUMPHANT RETURN ⚓

One of the stars of the 1978 tournament, Paolo Rossi of Italy, was the winner of the Golden Boot four years later in Spain. But then it was the first time he had appeared for the *Azzurri* in two years following a ban for match fixing. While on loan with Perugia in 1980, Rossi was accused of taking a bribe after scoring both goals in a 2–2 draw with Avellino. Although initially suspended for three years, a combination of the striker's protests and the Italian side's dire need for a marksman meant that the sentence was commuted to two years, ending conveniently in April 1982 – just two months before the start of the tournament.

⚓ ROUT ⚓

With civil war raging back home, it was perhaps understandable that El Salvador had other things on their mind rather than a World Cup finals group match against Hungary in 1982. Sadly, Hungary were in no mood for sympathy and won 10–1, a record in World Cup finals. Such was the dominance of the Hungarians that three of the goals were scored by Lazlo Kiss, who came on as a substitute after 55 minutes and duly wrapped up his hat-trick in seven minutes, another World Cup record.

⚑ GREAT GAMES: ENGLAND 3–2 CAMEROON (AET), 1990 ⚑

Having already reduced their supporters' nerves to shreds against Belgium, England once again put the Barmy Army through the wringer in what was expected to be a walk-over against Cameroon in the quarter-final. Platt gave them the lead on 25 minutes, but England were then comprehensively outplayed by the Africans who could have easily scored three goals in the first half. With the iconic Roger Milla on in the second, Cameroon scored twice in five minutes to put Bobby Robson's men on the brink of an ignominious exit. They were saved by an 83rd minute Lineker penalty which took the match into extra-time, then by a second Lineker spot-kick with just six minutes remaining. Cameroon were out, but England were lucky.

⚑ ROBSON'S RECORD BREAKER ⚑

After a shaky qualification, England weren't expected to set World Cup 1982 alight – especially when key players Kevin Keegan and Trevor Brooking were ruled out of the first-group match against France with injuries. Inspirational midfielder Bryan Robson had other ideas, however. With just 27 seconds on the clock, Robson latched onto a cross to hammer the ball into the net. It launched England on their way to a marvellous 3–1 victory and an unbeaten record in the group. But as so often, England had flattered to deceive. Having drawn against West Germany in the second-group phase, they needed to beat Spain by two clear goals to reach the semi-finals. Forced to field the clearly unfit Keegan and Brooking, England crashed out of the tournament following a nerve-wracking goalless draw.

⚑ BANNED CAPTAIN ⚑

Luigi Allemandi captained Italy in the 1934 World Cup – despite having been banned from the game for life after accepting a 50,000-lire bribe to throw a league match between Juventus and Torino. As one of their best players, the selectors decided it would be prudent to rehabilitate Allemandi rather than lose him for the finals.

⚓ ARMSTRONG POUNCES ⚓

In 1958 Billy Bingham played for Northern Ireland in the World Cup finals in Sweden, so after an absence of 24 years it was perhaps fitting that Bingham should be the manager to take the Irish to the finals in Spain. Few expected them to qualify from a strong group and, after a brave draw against Yugoslavia and a more fitful stalemate against Honduras, it was assumed their final match against the hosts would be their swansong in the competition. The Irish, though, had other ideas. In front of a partisan crowd of 50,000 in Valencia, Bingham's men were immediately under the cosh. Then, two minutes before half-time, Spanish keeper Arconada lethargically palmed away a cross by Billy Hamilton and there was striker Gerry Armstrong to lash home the rebound. Despite having Mal Donaghy sent off on the hour for retaliating to a crunching tackle by Camacho, the Irish somehow clung on for a win which against all the odds saw them through to the next phase as group winners.

⚓ THE PRINCE STEPS IN ⚓

Trailing 3–1 to a Michel Platini-inspired French team, the minnows of Kuwait were heading out of the 1982 World Cup. And that might well have been the last we heard of them, had it not been for an extraordinary incident after 76 minutes. With the Kuwaiti defence seemingly playing statues in the penalty area, Alain Giresse nipped in to make it 4–1 from close range. As Giresse celebrated, the Kuwaitis surrounded Soviet referee Stupar claiming that they had stopped after hearing a whistle. The situation exploded in to farce seconds later when none other than Prince Fahid, the Kuwaiti FA president, marched onto the pitch and demanded that the goal should be disallowed. For eight minutes a furious row took place in which the Prince threatened to take his players off the pitch and French boss Michel Hidalgo had to be restrained by the police when the referee subsequently reversed his decision.

With order finally, if unsatisfactorily, restored, the match restarted. France attacked and Bossis scored to make it 4–1 again. This time Prince Fahid had no cause for complaint – and it is unlikely the £8,000 fine from FIFA troubled his bank balance either.

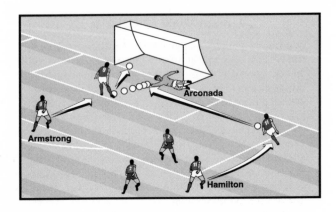

⚓ BRAZIL GOALS ⚓

Brazil lit up the 1982 World Cup finals in Spain with some extraordinary goals. Among the highlights were:

- Brazil 2–1 Soviet Union: Socrates equalises with a thunderous long-range shot before a swerving left-foot effort by Eder clinches the win.
- Brazil 4–1 Scotland: Zico bamboozles Rough with a viciously curling free-kick from the edge of the box before Eder leaves the Scottish keeper stranded with an exquisite lob.
- Brazil 4–0 New Zealand: Zico opens the scoring with an improbable bicycle kick straight into the back of the net.
- Brazil 3–1 Argentina: Eder's long-range free-kick dips and swerves before crashing off the underside of the bar for Zico to apply the finish. Junior then fires home after some sensational one-touch approach play which leaves the Argentines helpless.
- Brazil 2–3 Italy: Brazil bow out, but not before Falcao scores one of the goals of the tournament, wrong-footing the defence before driving home a magnificent left foot effort from the edge of the box.

⚓ IRELAND ELIMINATED ⚓

History repeated itself when Northern Ireland were eliminated from the 1982 finals in Spain thanks to a 4–1 defeat to France. In 1958, the last time the Irish appeared in the finals, they were knocked out by France, who scored four goals against them.

⚓ CAUSIO GETS HIS REWARD ⚓

With just minutes remaining in the World Cup final of 1982, and with his side leading West Germany 3–1, Italian manager Enzo Bearzot substituted goalscorer Altobelli and replaced him with Franco Causio, thus ensuring the veteran would receive a winners' medal.

⚓ COLOMBIA BALE OUT ⚓

Colombia was the original choice as venue for the 1986 World Cup finals, but when they couldn't raise the finances required FIFA moved the tournament to Mexico for the second time.

⚓ THE DEATH OF A LEGEND ⚓

The 20,000 Scottish fans who descended on Ninian Park for their side's World Cup qualifying match against Wales on 15 September 1985 were jubilant after Davy Cooper's 81st-minute penalty secured the draw they needed for Mexico. But on the touchline, manager Jock Stein had collapsed after an altercation with a photographer near the dug-out. Stein was rushed to the dressing room where, after an agonising wait of nearly twenty minutes, it was announced to a stunned crowd that the Big Man had died.

⚓ SMILE PLEASE, HUGO ⚓

Mexico's Hugo Sanchez, a star of the 1986 tournament, was not only a natural goalscorer, he was also a qualified dentist!

⚓ F-WORD ⚓

'Give me the f***ing ball!'
– Mild-mannered Ray Wilkins caught by a pitchside microphone berating a ball-boy during England's dismal 0–0 draw against Morocco in 1986

⚓ CRAZY COMMENTATOR ⚓

'There! He blew the whistle! Norway has beaten England 2–1 at football and we are the best in the world! England, the home of the giants! Lord Nelson! Lord Beaverbrook! Sir Winston Churchill! Sir Anthony Eden! Clement Atlee! Henry Cooper! Lady Diana! Maggie Thatcher! Can you hear me Maggie Thatcher? I have a message for you in your campaigning. As they say in the boxing bars around Madison Square Garden in New York, your boys took one hell of a beating. Your boys took one hell of a beating!'

– Norwegian commentator Bjorg Lillelien goes mental after his team of part-timers had beaten England 2–1 in a World Cup qualifier in 1981

⚓ REPEAT PERFORMANCE FROM HURST ⚓

As a fundraiser for victims of the Bradford fire disaster in 1985, members of the 1966 England World Cup-winning team arranged a match with their German counterparts at Elland Road, Leeds. This time England won 6–4 – and 46-year-old Geoff Hurst got another hat-trick.

⚓ ON YOUR BIKE, PEDRO ⚓

Fanatical Argentina supporter Pedro Garita was determined to see his team play in the 1986 World Cup in Mexico. Lacking the money for the airfare, he decided to travel there by bicycle. He arrived a month later, having covered 4,460 miles, in time for the final between Argentina and West Germany. Unfortunately, Pedro approached the ticket office to be told the match was a sell-out and had been for weeks. To make matters worse, as he trudged disconsolately outside, he discovered that someone had nicked his bike!

⚓ BIG JACK HEDGES HIS BETS ⚓

In 1990, the Republic of Ireland drew 0–0 with Egypt in a qualifying match. When asked which of the Egyptian players had impressed him, the Irish boss scratched his head: 'I couldn't tell you,' he said. 'I don't know their names. There was the boy with the beard, the dark lad in midfield, the keeper, the little dark lad who played centre-midfield, the very coloured boy, and the boy who played up front.'

⚓ THE POPE'S A FAN ⚓

'I know you!'
– Pope John Paul II makes a beeline to Irish manager Jack
Charlton during the squad's visit to the Vatican in 1990

⚓ BATISTUTA HAT-TRICKS ⚓

On 21 June 1994, Argentina striker Gabriel Batistuta scored a penalty to
complete a hat-trick against Greece, who were competing in their first World
Cup finals. On 21 June 1998 Batistuta scored a penalty to complete a hat-
trick against Jamaica, who were competing in their first World Cup finals.

⚓ UNPOPULAR HARALD ⚓

After his horror tackle on Patrick Battiston in the 1982
semi-final against France, West German goalkeeper
Harald Schumacher was voted the 'most unpopular
man in history' in a French newspaper poll. Adolf Hitler
came second.

⚓ BLUNDER SQUAD ⚓

Everyone likes to speculate on the all-time greatest World Cup
players – but what about the players who had the worst moments
in the World Cup? Here's a squad of unfortunates you wouldn't
like to see in your team colours.

Goalkeeper: Andoni Zubizaretta (Spain). Literally handed a 3–2
victory to Nigeria when a pair of blunders cost his team a second-
round berth in 1998.

Defenders: Jose Batista (Uruguay) received the fastest red card in
Cup history after 53 seconds in a 1986 match. Barmeer Shaker
(Iraq) was handed a one-year suspension for spitting at a referee
after a defeat to Belgium in 1986. Rigobert Song (Cameroon) is
the only player to be red carded in two Cups, in 1994 and 1998.

Midfielders: Ray Wilkins (England) was sent off for throwing the
ball at the referee during a match against Morocco in 1986.
Stefan Effenberg (Germany) was sent home after giving a one-
fingered salute to fans after a game in 1994. Ariel Ortega
(Argentina) was red carded for head-butting keeper Edwin Van
Der Sar, minutes before Holland's winning goal in 1998.

Forwards: Hugo Sanchez (Mexico) missed a penalty kick in a 1–1 draw with Paraguay in 1986 after he was featured in a TV commercial converting a kick. Gianluca Vialli (Italy) missed a penalty kick, had a goal disallowed due to offside and missed a sitter with an embarrassingly poor bicycle kick during a match against the USA in 1990.

Coach: Paraguay's Cayeteano Re became the first coach to be ejected from a match, in 1986. His crime? Standing too close to the field.

⚑ ZOLA'S BIRTHDAY ⚑

Italy striker Gianfranco Zola was hoping to celebrate his 28th birthday with a World Cup win against Nigeria in the 1994 finals. His side duly won 2–1, but Zola's happy day was soured when he was sent off after 76 minutes.

⚑ PREUD'HOMME'S SHIRT ⚑

During the 1994 finals in America Belgian goalkeeper Michael Preud'homme never forgot his roots, and underneath his international jersey always wore a Standard Liège shirt in homage to his first club and to bring him good luck. Unfortunately, having qualified for the knock-out phases, Preud'homme decided it was just too hot to wear two shirts and left his Liege jersey in the changing room for the match against Germany. Inevitably, the Germans put three goals past him to win 3–2.

⚑ ALBANIA SHIRTS ⚑

After a qualifying tie with Spain in 1993, Albania coach Bekjush Berce forbade his players from exchanging shirts. The reason was that the Albanian FA only had eleven shirts, and were so impoverished they couldn't afford a new set.

⚑ ROMANIA PLAY BY ROYAL APPOINTMENT ⚑

Romania's players attended the 1930 World Cup finals by royal command – literally. The team was hand-picked by soccer-mad King Carol II, who also ordered their employers to grant them three months leave on full pay.

⚓ EXTRA EXTRA-TIME ⚓

There were puzzled looks between the players of Italy and Argentina as the first half of extra time in their 1990 semi-final dragged on for 23 minutes. Nobody had been injured, there had been no hold-ups, so why didn't French referee Michel Vautrot blow his whistle? It was only when one of the Italian players posed the question that the embarrassed Vautrot realised he had been so engrossed in the match he had forgotten to look at his watch. Fortunately, no goals were scored in the extra-time of extra-time.

⚓ MEXICO BANNED ⚓

Mexico, hosts of the 1986 finals, were banned from the 1990 tournament in Italy after FIFA discovered they had fielded three over-age players in an international youth tournament.

⚓ SIX MINUTES ⚓

When Brazilian referee Almeida Rega blew for full-time in the 1930 match between Argentina and France, the South Americans were understandably jubilant. Not only were they clinging onto a 1–0 lead, but there were still six minutes to go. A red-faced Rega apologised and, half-an-hour later, brought the two sides back onto the pitch in order to play out the last six minutes. There were no further goals.

⚓ URUGUAY CAGED ⚓

Prior to staging the inaugural World Cup finals in 1930, the Uruguay squad were isolated in a Montevideo hotel for nearly eight weeks to ensure there were no distractions to their preparations. The regime proved too much for goalkeeper Antonio Mazzali, who staged a daring midnight break-out in order to visit his girlfriend.

⚐ ONE HAND CASTRO ⚐

Hector Castro of Uruguay scored the winning goal in the 1930 final, despite having lost a hand and part of his arm in a childhood accident.

⚐ NEW HOUSE ⚐

Each member of the victorious Uruguay team of 1930 was given a plot of land and a new house in Montevideo by their grateful government.

⚐ WASTED JOURNEY ⚐

After a sea journey of more than 6,000 miles, Mexico and the USA arrived in Rome for the 1934 World Cup finals to be informed they must play a qualifying match to see which of them actually qualified for the finals. Mexico lost 4–2 and went home immediately. The USA lasted precisely three days longer, when they were beaten by the hosts in the first game of the finals!

⚐ POLDI MAKES A SPECTACLE OF HIMSELF ⚐

Swiss centre-forward Poldi Keilholz was so short-sighted he had to wear spectacles when he played. Nevertheless this did not prevent him banging in three goals in two matches during the 1934 finals.

⚐ AWESOME ORSI SHOT ⚐

Italian winger Raimondo Orsi's freakishly curling shot in the 1934 final against Czechoslovakia was worthy of winning any World Cup final. In reality Orsi's goal was the dramatic last-gasp equaliser which took the match into extra-time which Italy went on to win. The following day, Orsi, accompanied by dozens of press photographers, returned to the stadium in order to reproduce the shot for posterity. Despite trying more than twenty times, however, the ball resolutely refused to find the back of the net. Eventually, Orsi gave up.

⚓ LEONIDAS STICKS THE BOOT IN ⚓

At the start of a 1938 finals match against Poland, Brazilian player Leonidas took off his boots because he wanted to play in the muddy pitch barefooted. The referee immediately ordered him to put his boots back on. The Polish players must have wished the ref had kept his mouth shut: Leonidas went on to score four goals in the match, and to finish top scorer in the competition with eight goals in four matches. It might have been more had he not been controversially rested for the semi-final against Italy – a match which the understrength Brazilians went on to lose 2–1.

⚓ BROTHERS IN MANAGEMENT ⚓

Brazil's 1954 manager Zeze and the side's 1962 boss Aimore Moreira are the only two brothers to have managed the same nation in World Cup finals.

⚓ PEPPINO'S SHORTS ⚓

Peppino Meazza of Italy was overjoyed to score a penalty in the 1938 World Cup semi-final. But his moment of glory quickly turned to humiliation when his shorts – which had been torn earlier in the match – gave up the ghost and fell to his ankles, revealing his bare backside to the capacity Rome crowd. Meazza's team-mates surrounded him, protecting his shattered modesty until a replacement pair could be brought onto the pitch.

⚓ WIN OR DIE ⚓

Before the 1938 World Cup final against Hungary, the Italian team were sent a telegram by their dictator Mussolini, urging them to 'Win...or Die!' Fortunately for Italy, they did indeed win.

⚓ NO BRITISH TEAMS ⚓

British teams declined to enter the World Cup finals until 1950. This was because in 1928 the four home associations had quit FIFA over a row about so-called 'broken time' payments to amateur players. They did not rejoin FIFA until 1946.

⚑ RIMET HIDDEN ⚑

To prevent the Nazis from stealing the Jules Rimet trophy during the war, the World Cup was kept in a shoebox under the bed of Dr Ottorino Barrassi, an Italian sports official and member of FIFA's ruling council.

⚑ ENGLAND DEFEAT IS VICTORY ⚑

Early editions of British newspapers reported that England had beaten the USA 10–1 in the 1950 finals, when in fact the Americans had recorded a stunning 1–0 win. The reason for the mistake was simple: sports editors refused to believe that England could have lost, and assumed the copy-takers had made a typing error.

⚑ WHAT EVER HAPPENED TO LARRY ⚑

Larry Gaetjens was born in Haiti, but became a hero in his adopted USA when he scored the goal which defeated England in the 1950 World Cup finals. Returning to Haiti after his career was over, Gaetjens became a political activist, and was responsible for organising several anti-government organisations. This eventually landed him in jail where, starved and tortured, he died.

⚑ IRON BAR ⚑

Making his way to the pitch for his country's match against Brazil in 1950, giant Yugoslav player Rajko Mitic smacked his head on an iron girder in a corridor of the half-built Maracana Stadium. With blood pouring from his wound, Mitic was taken away for stitches while the Yugoslav officials asked the referee to delay the kick-off by ten minutes. He refused, and so Yugoslavia took the field with just ten men. Brazil duly scored after three minutes. Despite a gallant rearguard action led by the heavily bandaged Mitic, the hosts ran out 2–0 winners.

⚑ HOLY DAY ⚑

Having qualified for the 1958 World Cup finals, Northern Ireland were very nearly scuppered by their own football association. Two of their pool games were scheduled to be played on Sunday which, the Northern Irish FA pointed out, was against Irish law. Incredibly, it took a vehement protest by the players themselves to persuade the FA to scrap the law and prevent the team being disqualified for not completing their matches.

⚱ LEONIDAS, P.I. ⚱

After becoming the top scorer in the 1938 finals, Brazilian striker Leonidas returned to Rio where he continued in his day job – as a private investigator.

⚱ IDENTITY CRISIS ⚱

The opening match of the 1966 World Cup between England and Uruguay suffered an administrative glitch because seven of the England team had left their identity tags at the hotel. A motorcycle dispatch rider was immediately sent back to get them.

⚱ SUDAN THROUGH ⚱

Despite both teams winning 4–2 in their qualifying matches, Sudan went through to the 1970 World Cup finals at Zambia's expense because of a FIFA directive that the team scoring more goals in the second leg – in this case Sudan – would go through. Unsurprisingly it was the first and only time this grossly unfair means of qualification was used.

⚱ RIVELINO STRETCHERED OFF ⚱

Having survived the clumsy challenges of clodhopping defenders to become one of the players of the 1970 World Cup, Brazil's Rivelino was eventually stretchered off the pitch at the end of the final against Italy – after being jumped on by his own jubilant supporters.

⚱ EYE FOR AN EYE ⚱

Having had his sight saved by an operation prior to the 1970 World Cup finals, Brazil's Tostao gratefully gave his winners' medal to his eye surgeon.

⚱ TWO CRACKERS BY JOSIMAR ⚱

For a player who was, according to the team sheet anyway, a full-back, Brazil's Josimar Pereira scored two of the best goals of the 1986 World Cup. His first came against Northern Ireland, and was a raking 25-yard drive which left 41-year-old Pat Jennings helpless. His second was even better: receiving the ball on the right against Poland, he dribbled through three tackles before blasting a viciously dipping shot over goalkeeper Mlynarczyk from a seemingly impossible angle.

⚓ FAMOUS LAST WORDS ⚓

After snootily claiming that the World Cup trophy would never be stolen in Brazil because its fans loved and respected the game too much, the Brazilian football authorities were left red-faced in 1983 when the Jules Rimet trophy, won in perpetuity in 1970, was duly nicked from a display cabinet at the BFA headquarters in Rio. It was never recovered – unlike in England, where Pickles the dog was the hero of the hour.

⚓ NEW TROPHY ⚓

Unlike the Jules Rimet trophy, the current FIFA World Cup trophy will not be given to the next team to win three tournaments. However, in 2038 all the space for the winners' names on the base of the trophy will have been used up – which means that the winners of the 2042 tournament will be the first to lift the new World Cup.

⚓ THE MADNESS OF EL LOCO ⚓

Known as El Loco ('The Madman'), Peru's goalkeeper Ramon Quiroga was well known for running out of his penalty area in order to help out his defence and, sometimes, his midfield. During a pool game against Poland in 1978, El Loco excelled even himself by racing fully 60 yards from his goal line and rugby-tackling winger Gzegorz Lato.

⚓ SCHUMACHER'S TACKLE ⚓

The semi-final of the 1982 World Cup between West Germany and France will be for ever remembered for an act of brutality which was only topped in the incredulity stakes by the refereeing decision which followed it. With 57 minutes played and the scores tied at 1–1, France's Patrick Battiston was sent clean through the German defence. Harald Schumacher, Germany's combative, permed goalkeeper came racing out of his goal and launched into Battiston in what can only be described as a kung fu-style assault. Battiston crashed to the turf, where he lay unconscious for three minutes, blood pouring from his mouth where three of his teeth had been knocked out (Spanish police had inexplicably banned the Red Cross from attending the game). Unsurprisingly, the French team were incensed, and even Schumacher himself seemed prepared for the inevitable dismissal. Yet, incredibly, Dutch referee Charles Corver not only declined to book the goalkeeper, but awarded the Germans a free-kick! Corver claimed not to have seen the incident – which would have made him the only one in the stadium.

⚑ LERBY'S PREVIOUS ENGAGEMENT ⚑

With his side cruising to a 4–1 victory in a qualifying match against the Republic of Ireland in Dublin in 1985, Danish midfielder Soren Lerby was substituted after 58 minutes. Instead of an early bath, however, Lerby was driven to the airport where he caught a private jet to Munich – where he was in time to come on as a substitute in his club Bayern's 1–1 draw against rivals Bochum.

⚑ ROOSTER BOOSTER ⚑

During a match between France and Canada in 1986, the referee was obliged to stop the match while a dead cockerel was removed from the pitch. It had been thrown there by Canadian fans.

⚑ SPITTING MAD ⚑

Iraqi defender Barmeer Shaker was banned for a year by FIFA after spitting at the referee following his side's 2–1 defeat to Belgium in 1986.

⚑ EVEN STEVENS ⚑

There were two players called Gary Stevens in the England side that played Paraguay in 1986. They were not related.

⚑ ESCOBAR ASSASSINATED ⚑

Scoring an own goal is unfortunate, but it is hardly a capital offence. Yet that is precisely what happened to Colombia defender Andres Escobar in 1994. Playing against the USA, Escobar stuck out a leg to clear a cross by Harkes and put it past his own goalkeeper. The US went on to win the game 2–1, and were eventually eliminated from the tournament. Nine days later, Escobar was leaving a restaurant in Medellin with his fiancée when he was attacked by three men. One of them said 'Thanks for the own goal' and repeatedly shot Escobar in the chest and face. As each bullet struck home the assailants shouted: 'Goal'. Over 100,000 Colombians attended his funeral. A few months later Humberto Munoz Castro, a chauffeur, was arrested for the shooting. He was alleged to be a hit-man acting for wealthy drug barons who had bet $20 million on Colombia beating the USA. On 30 June 1995, almost exactly a year after Escobar's own goal, Castro was jailed for 43 years.

⚐ PENALTY MISS ⚐

'The fifteenth World Cup ended as it began – with a risible penalty miss by a highly paid and vastly overrated superstar.'
– comment by an English journalist after Roberto Baggio had gifted the 1994 World Cup to Brazil. A month earlier, at the opening ceremony, former Supreme Diana Ross had also scuffed a choreographed penalty wide of the goal

⚐ WHO'S GOT THE BALL? ⚐

One of the great conundrums in the wake of the 1966 World Cup final was 'did the ball cross the line?' Another was: 'what actually *happened* to the ball?' It was generally assumed that as the scorer of a hat-trick, the ball was in the possession of Geoff Hurst. Not so. In the build-up to Euro '96, it transpired that it was actually in the attic of Helmut Haller, scorer of the first West German goal. 'It rolled towards me at the end and I picked it up,' Haller revealed. Thus began a concerted campaign by the English tabloid press to bring the ball back home. After several weeks of wrangling and underhand dealing, Haller and the ball were eventually smuggled into England by the *Daily Mirror*. The ball was placed at Waterloo Station and Haller was paid £70,000. Today the ball has pride of place at the National Football Museum in Preston.

⚐ SCOTLAND WON, ESTONIA DIDN'T TURN UP ⚐

The World Cup qualifier between Estonia and Scotland in 1996 had been scheduled to kick off in Talinn at 6.55 p.m. But when Scotland boss Craig Brown arrived at the ground he noticed the temporary floodlights were attached to the back of lorries and complained that they could dazzle his players. FIFA acted quickly and brought the kick-off forward to 3 p.m. This, however, did not impress the Estonian officials, who complained that not only would they be unable to get security staff in place so early but most of their own supporters would still be at work. As a result, when Scotland took to the field at 2.55 p.m., they were alone. Estonia had not turned up. Referee Miroslav Radoman dispensed with the coin-toss (in case Scotland's John Collins should call incorrectly), and duly blew his whistle to start the game. Billy Dodds passed the ball to Collins and then Radoman blew for full-time as the Scottish fans chanted 'Easy, easy' from the terraces.

Unfortunately, FIFA then decided that instead of awarding Scotland the points, they would be forced to replay the match at a neutral venue. This time it wasn't so easy, as Brown's men struggled to a 0–0 draw in Monaco four months later.

⚓ THE WORST TEAM IN THE WORLD ⚓

In 1998 France proved they were the best team in the world by beating Brazil 3–0 in the World Cup final. But the worst team in the world had been decided long before that famous night in the Stade de France. In their six-match qualifying campaign in the Asian Zone, the Maldives lost 17–0 and 9–0 to Iran, 12–0 twice to Syria, and 6–0 and 3–0 to Kyrgyzstan. Their record of P6, L6, D0, F0 A59 remains the worst in World Cup history.

⚓ WIN OR DIE ⚓

Iraq needed to win their match against Kazakhstan in order to qualify for the 1998 World Cup. Disastrously, they lost 2–1. The president of the Iraqi FA was Uday Hussein, psychopathic son of Saddam, and a man who did not take defeat lightly. According to the testimony of two Iraqi players who have since defected to the West, several of the team were taken to the notorious Radwaniya prison, where they were shaved, dragged across gravel and then immersed in vats of raw sewage. The rest of the team were repeatedly beaten on the soles of their feet until they could hardly walk. FIFA sent a delegation to investigate the claims, but unsurprisingly they found only people who spoke in glowing terms about Uday and his methods.

⚓ DEATH OF A PRINCESS ⚓

The funeral of Princess Diana was scheduled for 6 September 1997. So was Scotland's World Cup qualifier against Belarus at Aberdeen. But while the rest of Britain closed down for the day, Jim Farry of the Scottish FA was determined that it should be business as usual. A huge row developed over whether playing the match would be disrespectful to the Princess's memory, with even the Scottish players at odds with each other. Gary McAllister said he was quite willing to play the game while striker Ally McCoist made it clear that if he was selected for a match on Saturday he would be forced to pull out. Eventually, after unseemly pressure was brought to bear, Farry conceded and the game was played the following day. The kerfuffle did not seem to affect the Scots unduly, as they ran out 4–1 winners.

⚔ SHEARER ALMOST MAKES AN ARSE OF HIMSELF ⚔

BBC viewers were perplexed when, following England's 2–0 win over Tunisia in the 1998 World Cup, England boss Glenn Hoddle and star striker Alan Shearer were interviewed in the tunnel of Marseille's Velodrome stadium. While Hoddle appeared on screen, Shearer was strangely excluded, with viewers only able to hear his disembodied voice. It later transpired that Shearer had positioned himself in such a way that his head was covering the M of a large Marseille sign, while the 'ILLE' was out of shot – thereby ensuring that the word 'ARSE' was visible directly beside him.

⚔ ANTI-TERRORIST MEASURES ⚔

Such was the fear of terrorist attacks during the 2002 Japan/South Korea World Cup that extraordinary measures were put in place to ensure there would be no repetition of what had happened in New York the previous year. Anti-aircraft guns were installed inside the stadium at Seoul to prevent a terrorist spectacular during the opening match between France and Senegal, while a six-mile no-fly zone was installed around all the stadiums hosting matches. Meanwhile military forces in South Korea were put on a state of high alert and submarines and warships were deployed off the coast to thwart maritime attacks.

⚔ WHAT MIGHT HAVE BEEN? ⚔

In March 1998 police and security forces raided a number of houses in Belgium and arrested seven members of an Algerian terror group. They subsequently discovered a chilling plot to create death and mayhem at that year's World Cup finals in France. First, the England team were to be massacred on the pitch using biological weapons. At the same time a group of armed terrorists would burst into the hotel used by the USA team and shoot them as they watched the match. The atrocity was planned as a dual attack on Britain and America and, although it failed, it meant that security at World Cups would from that moment on become a primary concern of FIFA.

⚓ TAKE-AWAY CURRY ⚓

In 1998, ten Scotland fans following their team in Bordeaux spent £600 on a take-away order of lager and curry which they telephoned through to the Eye of the Tiger restaurant in Bournemouth. They then spent a further £800 on a charter flight to deliver it to Bordeaux. Restaurant boss Mustafa Aolad said: 'It was such a good order we'd have liked to have delivered it free – but unfortunately it was beyond our usual five-mile radius. We all support Scotland now.'

⚓ STRAIGHT TALKING ⚓

'Our youths copy our footballers, but the players seem to forget that braids embrace a sense of homosexuality in the developing world – and we certainly don't want that.'
– Nigerian culture minister Otumba Runshewe commenting on star player Taribo West's bright green pigtails sported at the 1994 World Cup finals

⚓ ROMANIANS PREFER BLONDS ⚓

For their final group game against Tunisia at the Stade de France in 1998, the entire Romanian team dyed their hair peroxide blond – except for the goalkeeper, who was bald. 'This is a bonding exercise and a lucky charm to carry us all the way to final,' explained coach Anghel Iordanescu. Fat lot of good it did them. After only managing to draw against Tunisia, the Romanians were sent packing in the knock-out stages by Croatia.

⚓ PO-FACED ALF ⚓

'Sit down and behave yourself.'
– Alf Ramsey's stern advice to England trainer Harold Shepherdson, who had leaped to his feet in excitement as Geoff Hurst banged home the third goal of the 1966 final

⚑ AUSSIES RUN RIOT ⚑

There have been many one-sided football games in World Cup history, but none to match the 31–0 drubbing handed out by Australia to little American Samoa at a qualifying match for the 2002 tournament. The first nine minutes were goalless, but then the floodgates opened. Goals were scored after 10, 12, 13, 14, 17, 19, 21, 23, 25, 27, 29, 32, 33, 37, 42 and 45 minutes. There then followed a 15 minute respite for half-time before the slaughter continued with goals on 50, 51, 55, 56, 58, 60, 65, 66, 78, 80, 81, 84, 85, 88 and 89 minutes. Striker Archie Thompson's personal tally of 13 goals beat both the World Cup record (7) and Full International record (10) for a single game. 'We're here as a learning process,' said American Samoa manager Tony Langkilde. 'Our players' average age is 18. The only way is forward.'

⚑ SAN MARINO SHOCKER ⚑

San Marino, the tiny landlocked enclave in Northern Italy, is not renowned for its footballing prowess. Indeed most of the World Cup records they hold are for record defeats. Yet on 17 November 1993 the team of part-timers wrote themselves in to the World Cup history books for all the right reasons. It's just unfortunate that their opponents that night were England. The game was a World Cup qualifier staged at FIFA's insistence in nearby Bologna. England, under Graham Taylor, were as good as doomed to sit out the 1994 finals, but insult was very quickly added to injury when Stuart Pearce's underhit back-pass was pounced on by Davide Gualtieri who hammered it into the net after just 8.3 seconds. Although the part-timers went on to lose 7–1, Gualtieri's goal was the quickest ever scored against England, and the fastest in a World Cup qualifier.

⚑ REFEREE IN TROUBLE ⚑

'It was me against 22. The game was uncontrollable. I wasn't reffing a football match, I was an umpire in military manoeuvres.'
– English referee Ken Aston, who officiated in the bloody 'Battle of Santiago' between Chile and Italy in 1962

⚑ SEEING YELLOW AND RED ⚑

Welsh referee Clive Thomas was known as a stickler for the rules, but he was not a patch on Russian official Valentin Ivanov, who took charge of the 2006 World Cup clash between Portugal and Holland. During the course of the game Nieto showed a whopping sixteen yellow cards and four red cards – a record for a finals match, but perhaps par for the course in a tournament in which there were 345 yellows and 28 reds.

WHO US, REF?

Antonio Rattin may have got his marching orders during the stormy World Cup quarter-final between England and Argentina in 1966, but both Bobby and Jack Charlton were booked. However, because this was the last tournament before the introduction of red and yellow cards, neither brother realised until the following day.

THE 12TH MAN

Shortly before his team's World Cup match against Portugal in 2002, a South Korean fan in the city of Pusan committed suicide by dousing himself in paint thinner and setting himself alight. It was only later, when his suicide note was discovered, that his reasons became clear:

'I am choosing death because South Korea has far to go to compete with Latin American and European teams. So I will be a ghost, the 12th player on the pitch, and do my best for the team.'

Did he succeed? In 2002 South Korea confounded all the experts by reaching the semi-finals of the World Cup, where they were only narrowly pipped 1–0 by Germany.

⚑ BAGGIO THE BUDDHIST ⚑

'Before the game, my spiritual master told me I'd be confronted with a lot of pressure and that everything would be decided at the last minute. I felt very relaxed as I took the penalty. I didn't realise it at the time, but my spiritual master's prediction was exactly right.'
– Italy's Buddhist striker Roberto Baggio tries to make the best of his horrendous penalty miss in the 1994 World Cup final

⚓ SURPLUS TO REQUIREMENTS ⚓

Ahn Jung-Hwan missed what appeared to be a crucial penalty in South Korea's quarter-final match against Italy in 2002. But with the game stuck at 1–1 in extra-time, the long-haired Ahn became an instant hero when he scored the winning 'Golden Goal' to put his side through to the semis. The Italians were not impressed, especially Luciano Gaucci, president of Ahn's Italian club Perugia, who immediately sacked the Korean. Gaucci claimed that it was not Ahn's goal which had annoyed him so much as his comments after the game. 'He said Korean football was superior to Italian football, when Italy is a footballing nation. We have treated him well with all our love, but his comments were offensive to me and the entire Italian nation.' Gaucci added: 'He was a phenomenon only when he played against Italy. I am a nationalist and I regard such behaviour not only as an affront to Italian pride but also an offence to a country which two years ago opened its doors to him. I have no intention of paying a salary to someone who has ruined Italian soccer.' However, Gaucci later changed his mind and reinstated Ahn to the squad after protests from his own supporters.

⚓ CAMEROON'S KIT ⚓

In 2002 Cameroon arrived in Japan and South Korea sporting a natty piece of kit: skin-tight, sleeveless shirts. Unfortunately for them, the stuffed shirts of FIFA's hierarchy ruled that because they didn't have sleeves they were vests – in contravention of the laws. Although Cameroon pointed out that they'd worn their vest shirts during the African Cup of Nations, FIFA were having none of it. Threatened with expulsion, Cameroon reluctantly obeyed and added sleeves to the ensemble.

⚓ LOTHAR'S RECORD ⚓

In attempting to clear the ball during a game against Mexico in 1998, Germany's Lothar Matthaus hit his own post and very nearly scored an own goal. Ironically, had the ball gone in it would have secured Matthaus a place in history as one of only three men to have scored in four successive World Cup tournaments. As it was, he would fail to score in 1998.

⚓ TIME DIFFERENCE ⚓

Due to the time difference between South Korea and California, in 2002 USA star striker Landon Donovan was able to play for his country in a losing World Cup quarter-final on Friday and for his team, San Jose, on Saturday.

⚓ RONALDO'S BAD-HAIR DAY ⚓

A major talking point of the 2002 semi-final between Brazil and Turkey was striker Ronaldo's bizarre hairstyle, which was shaved except for a prominent tuft at the front. It transpired that in a previous game, Ronaldo's son, Ronald, had thought his dad was defender Roberto Carlos. A quick once-over with the clippers left nobody in any doubt – although the little lad must have wished he'd kept his mouth shut.

⚓ WORST WORLD CUP ⚓

On the day of the 2002 World Cup final, the world's worst teams got together for a special match to celebrate their spectacular ordinariness. Montserrat, rated 203rd in the FIFA rankings, took a five-day trip to the Himalayan kingdom of Bhutan, rated 202nd. Bhutan won the game 4–0 in front of 15,000 fans – twice the population of Montserrat. Afterwards the two sides had a slap-up meal together and watched Brazil beat Germany on the TV.

⚓ DE BRITO'S HOWLER ⚓

Valdemar de Brito of Brazil became the first player to miss a penalty in a World Cup when he blazed wide during his team's 3–1 defeat against Italy in 1934. Another first of which de Brito was rather more proud was that he was the first scout to spot the potential of a young player called Edson Arantes de Nascimento – better known as Pelé.

⚓ WORLD CUP WILLIE ⚓

World Cup Willie, a lion-like character first unveiled in England in 1966, was the first ever World Cup mascot.

⚓ SHIRT SWAPPING ⚓

Although it dated back to 1954, the post-match practice of shirt-swapping was temporarily banned in 1986 because FIFA objected to the sight of bare chests on a football field.

⚓ GROUP OF DEATH ⚓

The term 'Group of Death' was first coined by the Mexican press in 1970 to describe Group 3, which consisted of England (reigning champions), Brazil (winners in 1958 and 1962), Czechoslovakia (finalists in 1962) and Romania.

⚓ 1–0 ⚓

1–0 is the most frequent score in World Cup matches.

⚓ COMMON NAME ⚓

The most common name in World Cup finals is Gonzales (or Gonzalez), which has featured fifteen times since 1930.

⚓ UNLUCKY LUXEMBOURG ⚓

Plucky Luxembourg have attempted – and failed – to qualify for every World Cup finals since 1934. They have participated in 92 qualifying matches, losing 88, scoring 45 goals and conceding 308. The only two teams they have ever beaten are Portugal (4–2 in 1961) and Turkey (2–0 in 1972).

⚓ SAN MARINO SUCCESS ⚓

San Marino's 1–0 win over Liechtenstein in a qualifying match for the 2006 World Cup in April 2004 was their first competitive win in 73 years.

⚡ WORLD CUP FIRSTS: MATCHES ⚡

First match: Mexico 1, France 4 in Montevideo, Uruguay, 1930.

First tied match: Italy 1, Spain 1 in Florence, Italy, 1934.

First match with extra-time: Austria vs France, 1934.

First final with extra-time: Italy vs Czechoslovakia, 1934.

First scoreless match: Brazil vs England in Stockholm, Sweden, 1958.

First match decided on penalty shoot-out: Semi-final between West Germany and France, 1982, in which the Germans won the shoot-out 5–4.

First final decided on penalty shoot-out: The 1994 final in which Brazil beat Italy 3–2 after a 0–0 tie.

First match played indoors: USA vs Switzerland at Pontiac Silverdome, Detroit, USA, 1994.

First match where a coach was sent off: Paraguayan coach Cayetano Re in a match against Belgium, 1986.

⚡ WORLD CUP FIRSTS: GOALS ⚡

First goal in World Cup: Lucien Laurent of France against Mexico in the 19th minute in the first World Cup match, 1930.

First penalty goal: Mexico's Manuel Rocquetas Rosas against Argentina, 1930.

First penalty goal in a final: Johan Neeskens of Holland against West Germany, 1974.

First hat-trick: Guillermo Stabile of Argentina in their 6–3 win over Mexico, 1930.

First extra-time goal: Austria's Anton Schall in the match against France, 1934.

First first-minute goal:
Emile Veinante of France in the 40th second of the match against Belgium, 1938.

First own goal: Ernst Loertscher of Switzerland against West Germany, 1938.

First goal by a substitute: Mexico's Juan Basaguren in the match against El Salvador, 1970.

First hat-trick by a substitute: Laszlo Kiss of Hungary in a match against El Salvador, 1982.

First Golden Goal: France's Laurent Blanc in the 113th minute in the second-round match against Paraguay, 1998.

⚐ YOU AGAIN? ⚐

Throughout its often troubled history, FIFA have always been able to rely on Brazil to turn up for the World Cup. In fact they have played 87 matches over the seventeen tournaments since 1930, more than any other country. No wonder they've won it more than anybody else!

⚐ NOT JUST BRAZIL ⚐

Ask anyone which team has appeared in the most finals in the World Cup, and they will most probably say Brazil. But that would be to forget about Europe's most tenacious silverware hunters, Germany. In fact both nations have appeared in seven finals:
Brazil in 1950, 1958, 1962, 1970, 1994, 1998, 2002 and Germany in 1954, 1966, 1974, 1982, 1986, 1990, 2002. Strangely, the 2002 final was the only one in which they appeared together.

⚐ BRAZIL WINNERS ⚐

Brazil have won 64 World Cup matches, more than any other nation. In 2002 they won seven on the trot, equalling the record held by Italy between 1934–8. Mexico, by contrast, hold the record for the most defeats with twenty. They have also lost the most consecutive matches, nine, between 1930 and 1958

⚐ IMPREGNABLE ITALY ⚐

In 1990, Italy went five matches – or 450 minutes – without conceding a goal, which is a World Cup record. The run took them through to the semi-final where they survived a further 67 minutes intact before conceding to Claudio Caniggia of Argentina. That goal took the match into extra-time and then penalties, in which Italy conceded four while only managing to convert three.

⚑ MARVELLOUS MATTHAUS AND MALDINI ⚑

Between 1982 and 1998 Germany's powerhouse mid-fielder Lothar Matthaus played an unrivalled 25 consecutive World Cup finals matches. During that time he won a winner's medal and a runner's up medal. However, the record for the most completed matches belongs to Italy's evergreen Paulo Maldini, who managed 23 without being substituted between 1990 and 2002.

⚑ EL CAPITANO MARADONA ⚑

A lesser-known record held by Argentina's Diego Maradona is that he captained his side sixteen times in World Cup matches.

⚑ SHILTS RECORD ⚑

England's goalkeeper Peter Shilton kept a record ten clean sheets in World Cup matches between 1982 and 1990. In 1982 he conceded just one, in 1986 he was beaten three times, and in 1990 he let in four – if you don't count the four West Germany scored in the penalty shoot-out. Eight goals in three World Cup tournaments – and England never went further than the semis.

⚑ STILL THE BOSS ⚑

While most countries are happy to give their coach at least one tilt at the World Cup before sacking him, Germany clearly believe that managerial consistency is the key to success. And who can argue? Between 1966 and 1978 Helmut Schoen led his side to four World Cups, two World Cup finals and one World Cup final victory.

⚑ AHEAD OF THE REST ⚑

Miroslav Klose of Germany scored five goals with his head during World Cup 2002 in Japan/South Korea, the most by any player in finals history.

⚓ SPOT-KICK KINGS ⚓

It always pays to have a top-notch penalty taker on your side. Four of Eusebio's nine goals in the 1966 World Cup were from the spot, a record equalled only by Robbie Rensenbrink of Holland in 1978.

⚓ COMEDY OF ERRORS ⚓

The USA's 3–2 win over Portugal in the 2002 finals was one of the big shocks in a competition in which the minnows generally acquitted themselves well. It was also the first time in World Cup history that a match featured two own goals. Already trailing by a fourth-minute goal, Portugal made life even more difficult for themselves when Jorge Costa put through his own net on 29 minutes. Leading 3–1 in the second half and seemingly cruising to victory, Jeff Agoos duly beat his own keeper to set up a nerve-wracking last twenty minutes for the Americans.

⚓ KOREAN NIGHTMARE ⚓

Pity poor Yung Hong Duk. As the last line of a largely non-existent South Korean defence, the goalkeeper was always going to be in for a torrid time at the 1954 World Cup. And so it proved. In just two matches he picked the ball out of his own net a record sixteen times as his side collapsed 9–0 to Hungary and 7–0 to Turkey.

⚓ GOALS, GOALS, GOALS ⚓

At times there have been questions about their defence, but Brazil's philosophy has always been that it doesn't matter how many they score as long as we score more. Reckless perhaps – but with 201 goals between 1930 and 2002, the South Americans are by far the most prodigious finishers in World Cup history.

⚓ NUMBERS UP ⚓

The 1938 finals in France was the first time numbers were used on players' shirts in the World Cup.

⚐ GERMAN EFFICIENCY? ⚐

They are renowned for their defensive qualities and, in Franz Beckenbauer, possessed perhaps the World Cup's most complete defender. Yet amazingly Germany (and West Germany) have conceded 112 goals in their World Cup finals appearances – more than any other country. Fourteen of those goals were conceded over six matches in 1954, the year they first won the Jules Rimet trophy. Mind you, Germany have played more matches than anyone else apart from Brazil.

⚐ ALLEZ LES BLEUS AND MODERN CATENACCIO ⚐

In winning the World Cup on home turf in 1998, France conceded just two goals – at that time, the fewest by any World Cup-winning side. This record was subsequently equalled by a similarly mean-spirited Italian defence, led by FIFA World Player of the Year Fabio Cannavaro, during the 2006 World Cup.

⚐ RED AND YELLOW CARDS ⚐

Peru's captain Mario de Las Casas became the first player to be sent off in World Cup history when he was given his marching orders in a match against Romania in 1930. However, the first player to receive the red card was Chile's Carlos Caszely in a match against West Germany 44 years later. The first yellow had been shown to Lovchev of the USSR in 1970, again against West Germany.

⚐ THE SCORPION STUNG ⚐

Following in a long tradition of lunatic South American goalkeepers, Colombia's Rene Higuita earned himself a place in the history books in 1990 when, for reasons better known to himself, he decided to dribble the ball all the way from his own penalty area to the halfway line. As his team-mates watched open-mouthed, Higuita was duly dispossessed by Cameroon's Roger Milla who gleefully ran off and scored.

⚱ BORN WINNERS ⚱

The only European players to have won two World Cups are Italy's Giuseppe Meazza and Giovanni Ferrari, who both played in the 1934 and 1938 champion teams. Meanwhile the only player to have won three World Cups is the peerless Pelé of Brazil, who gained winners medals in 1958, 1962 and 1970.

⚱ BROTHERS WHO HAVE PLAYED IN WORLD CUP FINALS ⚱

Juan and Marino Evaristo of Argentina (1930)
Fritz and Ottmar Walter of West Germany (1954)
Jack and Bobby Charlton of England (1966)
Rene and Willy Van der Kerkhof of Holland (1978)

⚱ OTHER SIGNIFICANT EVENTS IN WORLD CUP YEARS ⚱

1930: First Empire Games held in Hamilton; Vannevar Bush and a team of scientists develop the 'Differential Analyzer', arguably first modern computer; planet Pluto discovered.

1934: Austrian Nazis murder Austrian Chancellor Dollfuss; Adolf Hitler combines positions of Chancellor and President, and becomes 'Führer' of Germany; 'Night of the Long Knives'.

1938: Civil War in Spain ends; German troops invade Austria; Orson Welles' broadcast of *War of the Worlds* causes panic across the USA; Lazlo Biro invents the ballpoint pen.

1950: Korean War begins; Florence Chadwick swims the Channel in 13 hours 22 minutes; comic strip *Peanuts* is published in the USA, featuring Good Ol' Charlie Brown; Shirley Temple retires from showbiz.

1954: *Fellowship of the Ring* is published, beginning the *Lord of the Rings* trilogy; Brown vs Board of Education of Topeka goes before the Supreme Court resulting in the end of racial segregation; Roger Bannister runs the four-minute mile; *Playboy* is first published.

1958: The Treaty of Rome marks the foundation of the European Economic Community; the Munich air disaster kills 21, including seven Manchester United players; Nikita Khrushchev becomes Soviet premier; the first parking meters are introduced in the UK.
1962: John Glen becomes the first American to orbit the Earth; the Rolling Stones make their debut in London; the Cuban missile crisis

brings the world to the brink of war; the Big Freeze hits the UK, with sub-zero temperatures until March 1963.

1966: Indira Ghandi of India becomes the first woman Prime Minister; John Lennon claims the Beatles are 'more popular than Jesus'; first episode of *Star Trek* is aired; a landslide in Aberfan, Wales, kills dozens of schoolchildren.

1970: Four students are shot dead by guardsmen at Kent State University; the Beatles split; Jimi Hendrix dies of a drugs overdose; General de Gaulle of France dies.

1974: President Nixon resigns due to his involvement in the Watergate scandal; kidnap attempt on Princess Anne in the Mall fails; Lord Lucan disappears.

1978: The film *Grease* is released; Louise Brown, the first test tube baby, is born; Bishop Karol Wojtyla of Poland becomes Pope John Paul II; the People's Republic of China lifts its ban on Shakespeare and Charles Dickens.

1982: The Falklands War breaks out; Kielder Water, the man-made lake, opens in Northumberland; Michael Fagan breaks into the Queen's bedroom; King Henry VIII's flagship *Mary Rose* is raised from the Solent after 400 years.

1986: The space shuttle *Challenger* explodes; Swedish prime minister Olaf Palme is shot dead; Prince Andrew marries Sarah Ferguson; fire breaks out at the Chernobyl nuclear reactor in the Ukraine.

1990: McDonald's opens a branch in Moscow; Nelson Mandela is released from captivity in South Africa; Poll Tax riots break out in London; the first Gulf War breaks out when US and coalition forces invade Iraq.

1994: The Church of England ordains its first women priests; ice skater Tonya Harding is convicted of organising an attack on her rival Nancy Kerrigan; Nirvana singer Kurt Cobain shoots himself; racing driver Ayrton Senna is killed.

1998: US President Bill Clinton is embroiled in the Monica Lewinsky sex scandal; Dana International, a transsexual from Israel, wins the Eurovision song contest; internet search engine Google is started.

2002: US troops invade Afghanistan; the Queen Mother dies; the Queen celebrates her Golden jubilee.

2006: The first case of bird flu is discovered in the UK; Lordi win the Eurovision Song Contest; Al Qaeda leader Abu Musab al-Zarqari is killed in Iraq; Google buys YouTube for $1.65 billion.

⚓ VOODOO CHILD ⚓

Before the 1974 tournament in West Germany, Haiti revealed their secret weapon for World Cup success: voodoo. However, the use of a witch doctor didn't help their cause, as they lost 3–1 to Italy, 7–0 to Poland and 4–1 to Argentina.

⚓ HAITI ⚓

Knowing that Papa Doc Duvalier was watching from the stands and understandably fearing for his safety should the home side lose, the referee in the World Cup qualifier between Haiti and visitors Trinidad contrived to disallow four perfectly good Trinidad goals as Haiti went on to win 2–1 and qualify for the 1974 finals in West Germany.

⚓ THE FIRST WORLD CHAMPIONS? ⚓

After beating English FA Cup winners West Bromwich Albion 4–1 at Hampden Park, Glasgow in a friendly match in 1888 – nearly 30 years before the first World Cup in Uruguay – Scottish Cup winners Renton declared themselves 'Champions of the United Kingdom and the World' and even had a trophy made to reinforce the fact. Such success did not last long, however. The following season the World Champions fell into financial difficulty and were forced to drop out of the league.

⚓ CAFÉ CULTURE ⚓

Belgium's star player Raymond Braine was suspended from the whole of the 1930 tournament – by his own football association. His crime? Opening a café!

⚜ WEST AUCKLAND WIN THE WORLD CUP ⚜

In 1909 tea magnate Sir Thomas Lipton decided to organise a 'world football tournament' to be held in Turin, Italy. But when he approached the FA about sending a team, they refused. Undeterred, Lipton chose West Auckland Town, a team consisting mostly of miners which was languishing third from bottom of the Northern Amateur League (it is thought one of the main reasons for choosing them was because their initials, WAFC, were the same as Woolwich Arsenal). Having sold most of their possessions to finance their trip, West Auckland not only took part in the four-team competition, but won it, beating Stuttgarter Sportfreund of Germany and FC Winterthur of Switzerland in the final to lift the 'Crown of Italy World Cup'. Not only that, but two years later the lads from County Durham did it again, this time beating the mighty Juventus 6–1 in the final. For this they were allowed to keep the trophy in perpetuity, and it remained behind the bar of West Auckland social club until 1994 when, like all good World Cup trophies, it was stolen.

⚜ NORTH KOREA NOT WELCOME ⚜

English fans took the North Koreans to their hearts in 1966 – but not the British government. Documents released 30 years later revealed how the prospect of communists on English soil filled the Foreign Office with dread. Among the secret moves to get them kicked out of the tournament were banning them entrance visas to the UK. When this didn't work, a plan was put into force designed to 'minimise the visual presence' and 'avoid doing anything where possible which might imply a diplomatic acceptance of the regime'. This included insisting that the team play as 'North Korea' and not the Democratic People's Republic of Korea, not inviting them to the World Cup draw, restricting Royal attendance to their matches and, unusually, banning the playing of national anthems except at the opening ceremony and the final. The North Koreans were also despatched to Middlesbrough and Liverpool to play their matches – a move which backfired spectacularly when the natives decided that the spirit of football was far more important than Cold War politicking.

⚓ POLICE ASSISTANCE ⚓

In the 1930 semi-final between Uruguay and Yugoslavia, the host's third goal in their 6–1 rout was scored after the ball ran out of play – and was neatly sidefooted back on by a uniformed policeman patrolling the touchline. All of the officials pretended not to notice, but then again the referee was Brazilian Gilberto Rega, who had already made a name for himself by ending the France vs Argentina match six minutes early by mistake.

⚓ ITALY QUALIFY ⚓

In 1934 FIFA decided that in the interests of fairness, even the nominated host country, Italy, should have to qualify for the finals. It seems not to have occurred to them what might have happened if the Italians had lost their vital play-off against Greece. Fortunately the Italians were not prepared to let that happen. After beating Greece 4–0 in Milan, they successfully 'persuaded' their opponents that the second leg was not necessary. To do this, the Italians funded and built a new headquarters for the Greek FA in Athens on the understanding that they would concede the game.

⚓ THE SAAR ⚓

Having spent most of its existence being passed between neighbours France and Germany, in 1953 the tiny principality known as The Saar was enjoying one of its rare periods of independence. To celebrate this, they applied to take part in the 1954 World Cup finals and were duly entered into a qualifying group which included Norway and West Germany. Amazingly, The Saar beat Norway 3–2 – but their dreams of performing on the World Cup stage were destroyed by the Germans who not only beat them but later rubbed salt into the wound by reassimilating them.

⚓ BLIND BALLOT ⚓

FIFA's intransigence about its rules reached farcical proportions in 1954 when, despite a 4–2 lead on aggregate over two legs, Spain were forced to play a decider against Turkey on neutral ground in Rome's Olympic Stadium for the right to reach the finals themselves. When this match finished 2–2, it was decided to draw lots to see who would go through. In order to ratchet up the tension a fourteen-year-old boy called Luigi Franco Gemma was brought out onto the pitch, blindfolded, and in front of a 40,000 crowd, asked to select one name from a large drum. Almost inevitably the name he selected was Turkey – which meant that despite winning 6–4 on aggregate, Spain were eliminated from the 1954 World Cup.

⚑ ROMARIO LOTHARIO ⚑

Brazil striker Romario claimed that during the 1994 World Cup he slept with no fewer than three women a day.

⚑ SUN TRAP ⚑

After 23 minutes of their 1954 quarter-final tie against Austria in Lausanne, hosts Switzerland were cruising at 3–0. Yet by half-time the Austrians had staged a remarkable recovery to lead 5–4. Perhaps embarrassed by the ease and swiftness with which the Austrians had regained the initiative, the Swiss officials came up with a novel excuse. A hastily drafted release was circulated in the press box claiming that 'All goals scored against Switzerland owing to the sun'. The sun did not bother the Austrians in the second half, as they added two more goals to run out convincing 7–5 winners.

⚑ JUST PERFECT ⚑

'I don't think anyone will beat my thirteen in a tournament. It is a record I will take to my grave.'
– France striker Just Fontaine who bagged a baker's dozen in the 1958 tournament in Sweden.

⚑ CRICKET STARS ⚑

West Indian cricket legend Viv Richards played for Antigua and Barbuda in their 1974 World Cup qualifying campaign. Meanwhile umpire Steve Bucknor, known as Slow Death for his deliberate raising of the finger, started his officiating career as a football referee. In 1988 he took charge of the 1990 qualifying match between El

Salvador and Netherlands Antilles. It was his only match at that level, as at the age of 45 he was obliged to stand down by FIFA. He went on to umpire in four cricket World Cup finals.

⚓ DUCK, PAL ⚓

Sometimes those training ground moves work out a treat. Such was the case in 1974, when the below-par Brazil team nevertheless produced a moment of magic against East Germany. Awarded a free-kick on the edge of the box, Jairzinho carefully took up position in the German wall. Up stepped Rivelino, whose powerful shot was aimed directly at his team-mate. On cue Jairzinho ducked and the ball flew into the back of the net.

⚓ ZAIRE HOWLER ⚓

A 9–0 hammering at the hands of Yugoslavia in their group match in 1974 suggested that Zaire were one of the World Cup's more hopeless competitors. In their next match against Brazil, the Africans revealed that they knew as much about the laws of the game as they did about defending. Brazil were awarded a free-kick on the edge of the box, but before Rivelino could take it, Zaire defender Mwepu sprinted from the wall and booted the ball away. Booked for his trouble, Mwepu explained later that he had seen other teams do it.

⚓ FLUMMOXED ⚓

At first it seemed that Scotland's World Cup woes had reached farcical proportions, but when Graeme Souness and Frank Gray appeared to run into each other as the Scots prepared to take a free-kick against New Zealand in their opening group match of the 1982 finals, laughter turned to roars of appreciation as John Robertson used the clever diversion to curl the dead ball into the back of the net past a distracted defence.

⚓ RED FACE FOR YELLOW CARD POLL ⚓

Referee Graham Poll was selected to officiate at the 2006 finals because, allegedly, he was the top whistleblower in England. His

World Cup pedigree was decidedly patchy, however. In 2002 he disallowed two perfectly good Italian goals during a 2-1 defeat to Croatia – and four years later, he very nearly did the Croatians another favour in their crunch Group F clash against Australia. Defender Josip Šimunic had already been booked once when he committed another blatant foul. Poll duly reached for his pocket – and produced another yellow. Despite the error being pointed out in no uncertain terms by the Socceroos, Poll, who had already sent off two players, maintained he was right. Four minutes later, when Šimunic committed yet another bookable offence, he was duly given a red card. The match finished 2-2, and the Aussies managed to scrape through to the knockout stage. But it was too late for the hapless Poll, who was himself booked – on the next plane home.

⚓ MARADONA ON THE SLIDE ⚓

As a player Diego Maradona scored some pretty crucial World Cup goals for Argentina. But the arguably the most important goal in the Albiceleste's illustrious history was scored with Maradona as manager. After a wretched qualifying campaign for the 2010 finals, Argentina found themselves needing to beat Peru in their penultimate match to at least give them a chance of going through by beating Uruguay in the final group game. They duly took the lead, but when Peru equalised in the 90th minute it seemed the unthinkable was about to come true. Then, in the third minute of stoppage time, veteran midfielder Martin Palermo was in the right place to fire home a dramatic winner. Maradona, famous for his energetic goal celebrations as a player, surpassed himself by joyfully sliding fully twenty yards along the touchline.

⚓ THE HAND OF HENRY ⚓

Thirteen years after Maradona's infamous "Hand of God" goal against England, the World Cup was rocked by yet another incident of blatant handball. This time the victims were the Republic of Ireland, who were playing France in a nerve-jangling play-off for the 2010 finals. With the scores level at 1-1 in extra time, and the match in Paris heading for penalties, the ball squirted through to Thierry Henry on the byline. Henry, renowned as one of the finest and fairest players ever to grace a football pitch, clearly used his hand to control the ball not once but twice before squaring for William Gallas to blast home the winner. Neither referee Martin Hansson nor his assistants saw the incident – and despite everybody in the stadium seeing the foul on the big screen replays, the goal stood and the Irish were out.

⚖ YOU HAVE TO HAND IT TO THE BEAUTIFUL GAME ⚖

"You have to take a philosophical approach to this match. Football is played on small details, however, qualification is still beautiful."
– French Football Federation president Jean-Pierre Escallettes has little sympathy for the Republic after Thierry Henry's handball.

⚖ JOSÉ PEKS THE WRONG MAN ⚖

When Argentina destroyed Serbia and Montenegro 6-0 in a scintillating display of attacking football during the 2006 group stages, it seemed we were not only watching the World Champions elect but, in young Lionel Messi, a worthy successor to the great Diego Maradona. But we all reckoned without the aptly-named Argentine coach José Pekerman, who pretty much single-handedly scuppered his own team's chances in the quarter final against Germany by leaving the brilliant Messi on the bench and substituting his other star player, Juan Riquelme, with the score just 1-0 to the South Americans. The Germans duly equalised and then, as usual, went on to win on penalties. Stunned, the Argentines kicked off a mini riot on the pitch, with players and officials joining in the sorry free-for-all.

⚖ GOODBYE TO ALL THAT ⚖

Seventy years after it hosted the 1936 Olympic Games, the Olympiastadion in Berlin was the natural choice as venue for the 2006 World Cup Final. It was here, of course, that Adolf Hitler saw the great Jesse Owens win four gold medals – and its historic significance was not lost on the architects responsible for redesigning it at a cost of □242 million. In particular the iconic stone towers at the entrance remained a focal point, despite many Germans wanting the whole structure torn down. According to interior minister Otto Schily, the stadium recalled "all the dark elements present in its creation. But in 2006 the world will look upon to modern, democratic, and open Germany."

⚓ GREAT GAMES: ARGENTINA 2-1 MEXICO, 2006 ⚓

In a tournament sorely lacking in quality, goals or indeed excitement, this all-South American second round clash had it all.

Argentina, with the likes of Riquelme, Crespo, Tevez and the mercurial 18-year-old Lionel Messi in the squad, were the red hot favourites to progress to the quarter finals, having played with joyous abandon and deadly intent during the group stage. Mexico, meanwhile, had stuttered through with a string of unimpressive performances against weak opposition.

A crowd of 43,000 in Leipzig sat back to watch the inevitable slaughter – but the Mexicans were determined they were not there to make up the numbers. Rocked by a series of pulsating attacks the Argentines were floored after just eight minutes when, from a wide free kick, Rafael Marquez stole in at the back post to smash the ball into the roof of the net.

Normal service appeared to have been resumed five minutes later when Mexico's Borghetti bundled a corner into his own net to level the scores. But despite thrills, spills and chances galore at both ends the match was still tied after 90 minutes – and it would take a goal of stunning quality to settle matters.

It came eight minutes into extra time when Argentina's Maxi Rodriguez, controlling an innocuous-looking ball on the corner of the Mexico penalty area, swung his left boot and volleyed an absolute peach into the far corner of the net. It was one of the goals of the tournament, and a fitting way to decide its best game.

⚓ GOALS OF THE TOURNAMENT, 2006 ⚓

It was not a vintage World Cup by any stretch of the imagination, yet the 2006 tournament nevertheless produced a number of stunning goals. These were the best 10, as chosen by the BBC pundits in Germany.

- PHILIPP LAHM, for Germany against Costa Rica: The opening goal of the tournament is a screamer as Lahm cuts in from the left wing and fires a thunderbolt from the corner of the box into the far corner of the net.
- TORSTEN FRINGS, for Germany against Costa Rica: What a game! What a goal! Midfielder Frings tries his luck from 35 yards – and nearly bursts the back of the net.
- TOMÁŠ ROSICKÝ, for Czech Republic against the USA: Another long range belter as Rosický hits it first time from 40 yards to give the sprawling Brad Friedel no chance.
- FERNANDO TORRES, for Spain against Ukraine: Spain's golden boy puts the finishing touch to a splendid, interpassing move masterminded by midfielder Puyol that cuts the Ukraine to shreds.
- STEVEN GERRARD, for England against Trinidad & Tobago: England are dismal, but Stevie G provides a moment to savour when he cuts in from the right and unleashes a 20-yard rocket into the top corner.
- ESTEBAN CAMBIASSO, for Argentina against Serbia & Montenegro: Argentina are simply sublime as they destroy their European opponents. Here Cambiasso fires home after a move consisting of 27 passes.
- BAKARY KONÉ for Ivory Coast against Holland: Individual genius as Koné picks up the ball on the halfway line, sets off on a scintillating run and beats four men before smashing it into the net from the edge of the box.
- DECO for Portugal against Iran: The magical Luis Figo weaves infield from the left wing before setting up Deco for a sublime 25-yarder that gives the Iranian keeper no chance.
- JOE COLE for England against Sweden: Another moment of brilliance in a tournament to forget for Sven's men. Cole controls a loose Swedish clearance before sending a looping, unstoppable volley fully 35 yards over the keeper's head.
- MAXI RODRIGUEZ for Argentina against Mexico: A stunning volley from the corner of the box was a fitting winner in this breathtaking second round clash.

⚓ HOT SHOT HIT LIST ⚓

Here's a list of the bookies' favourites to top the scoring charts in South Africa:

David Villa [SPA]: The Spanish hit man bagged three in 2006 and went one better to become top scorer in Euro 2008. At 28 he is now in his prime and will spearhead the thrilling Spain team.

Luís Fabiano [BRA]: The latest in a long line of brilliant Brazilian strikers, Fabiano scores for fun, including a hat-trick against Portugal in 2008. Last year he was top scorer in the Confederations Cup, including two goals in the final against the USA.

Fernando Torres [SPA]: If Villa doesn't score, Torres surely will. He's been on fire for Liverpool and, after a spell of injury, South Africa should see him at his best once again.

Wayne Rooney [ENG]: Top scorer in the qualifiers, Rooney has been world class since he was 17. With England buoyant under boss Fabio Capello, this could well be his year.

Cristiano Ronaldo [POR]: A controversial figure in 2006, Rooney's former strike partner went on to have his best domestic season ever. Now with Real Madrid he has a chance to prove he's got what it takes on the world stage.

Lionel Messi [ARG]: On his day the best player in the world – and those days are now a regular occurrence. Able to score them and set them up, Messi, still 22, will surely set South Africa alight.

Sergio Agüero [ARG]: Lethal finisher who has stepped seamlessly into Hernán Crespo's shoes, it would have been a travesty if Argentina's travails had prevented him from performing in South Africa.

Miroslav Klose [GER]: Solid, unglamorous, but nevertheless a goal machine. A centre forward from the old school, Klose is the current holder of the Golden Boot.

Nilmar [BRA]: A compact, effective goalscorer, Nilmar broke English hearts when he scored the winner for Brazil during a friendly at Wembley – and could do the same to most teams.

Robin van Persie [HOL]: Along with Cesc Fabregas, van Persie has revitalised Arsenal in the Premier League with his skills and his goals. Without him, Holland simply do not function.

Luca Toni [ITA]: Like Klose, Toni is a lumbering target man. But, like the German, he also gets his fair share of goals. He's due a good tournament.

Didier Drogba [IVO]: He's been lethal for Chelsea and, if he can keep his fragile temperament under control, he will prove a handful for the very best defences at World Cup 2010.

⚓ RONALDO'S A WINKER ⚓

England's stuttering 2006 World Cup campaign came to a merciful end when Portugal beat them on penalties following a fractious goalless draw in Gelsenkirchen. Apart from yet another shoot-out calamity for England, the game was marked by the sending off of the frustrated Wayne Rooney for appearing to stamp on Ricardo Carvalho. As Rooney tramped from the pitch, his Manchester United team-mate Cristiano Ronaldo was seen to wink knowingly at the Portuguese bench – suggesting that not only was getting under the England player's skin a tactic, but that it had succeeded perfectly.

⚓ RED CARD ARGIE ⚓

The referee who sent off Wayne Rooney was the Argentine Horacio Elizondo. Eight days later he would wave a red at Zinedine Zidane for his headbutt on Marco Materazzi in the World Cup Final.

⚓ HAT-TRICK OF SHAME ⚓

Wayne Rooney's sending off against Portugal made him the third English player to receive his marching orders during a World Cup match. He joined Ray Wilkins (1986) and David Beckham (1998) who also saw a direct red card in a World Cup encounter; the former for throwing the ball at the referee during a group game vs. Morocco, and the latter for petulantly kicking out at Argentinian midfielder Diego Simeone.

⚐ BIG PHIL'S INDIAN SIGN ⚐

England's defeat by Portugal meant they had been eliminated by a Luiz Felipe Scolari-led side in the last three major tournaments (Brazil, 2002; Portugal in 2004 and 2006, both on penalties).

⚐ SPORT FOR ALL ⚐

In 1936, the Olympics were broadcast across Berlin on 25 screens in selected venues across the city, the first time a major sporting event had ever been televised live. In 2006 fans who couldn't get a ticket for the Olympiastadion were able to enjoy the action on a 100 sq metre screen in a 20,000 capacity open-air amphitheatre just outside the ground.

⚐ BACK OF THE NETZER! ⚐

Former West German midfielder Günter Netzer was a 1970s legend who went on to become an equally popular TV pundit. During the 2006 semi-final between France and Portugal in Munich, he proved he had lost none of his old skills when the ball was kicked towards the his commentary position. Netzer calmly stood and headed the ball back onto the pitch, then turned to fellow pundits Marcel Desailly and Leonardo and said, "I've always wanted to do that."

⚐ OP ED ⚐

"England: like the New York Mets. Massively, ridiculously overrated by their media, always involved in some sort of comic downfall, insane injuries, woeful management. A car crash waiting to happen, at which stage the local media go berserk."
– US newspaper the Boston Globe pulls no punches in its assessment of Sven-Göran Eriksson's 2006 hopefuls.

⚑ PENALTY PUT-OFF ⚑

There can be fewer more nerve-racking moments in a player's career than taking a penalty in the World Cup finals. Pity Sweden's Henrik Larsson, then, who was just about to take a vital spot kick against Germany in the opening match of the 2006 tournament, when his manager Lars Lagerbäck decided to make a substitution. His concentration shot, Larsson duly fluffed the kick. Sweden duly lost the match 2-0.

⚑ A WORD FROM OUR SPONSORS ⚑

The 2006 tournament was the most commercial yet in terms of sponsorship from major global brands. But things reached a surreal stage when Dutch fans were told to remove their trousers if they wanted to watch the match against Argentina for fear of offending one of the big companies. More than 1,000 fans, sporting orange lederhosen supplied by Dutch brewer Bavaria, had to sit in their underpants on the orders of official sponsor Anheuser Busch, manufacturer of rival Budweiser beer.

⚑ RED LIGHT RECRIMINATIONS ⚑

It wasn't just football fans gearing up for a month of action in Germany. Hundreds of prostitutes from across Europe flooded into Berlin, Cologne and Munich, expecting to make a mint from the massed ranks of sex-crazed male supporters. But they were to be disappointed, as the predicted boom-boom time failed to materialise. Many of the women left before the quarter finals, with one Russian hooker bitterly criticising "stupid, wet men."

⚑ LEADING LEAGUES ⚑

Leagues with most players in the 2006 World Cup:
- England - 104
- Germany - 73
- Italy - 60
- France - 57
- Spain - 52

⚓ TOP TEN OR MORE ⚓

Here's a run down of the clubs who had ten or more players in World Cup Squads in 2006:

Chelsea - 15 players (subsequently increased to 17)
Arsenal - 15 players (subsequently increased to 16)
AC Milan - 13 players (subsequently reduced to 12)
Barcelona - 12 players
Juventus - 12 players
Manchester United - 12 players
Bayern Munich - 11 players (subsequently reduced to 10)
Dynamo Kiev - 10 players
Real Madrid - 10 players

⚓ BARMY UZBEKS ⚓

The award for shooting yourself in the foot goes to Uzbekistan, who, during a 2005 Asian group qualifying game against Bahrain, were awarded a penalty and duly scored it – despite a number of Bahrain players straying into the box. For some reason, however, they were incensed that Japanese referee Toshimitsu Yoshida had refused to order the spot-kick to be retaken, even though the goal had earned the Uzbeks a 1-0 win. The matter was referred to FIFA, who took the unusual step of ordering the match to be replayed. Bahrain gleefully won the match, and Uzbekistan were eliminated from the tournament.

⚓ DOCTOR ON CALL ⚓

Prior to the 2006 tournament Ecuador were taking no chances, and flew a witchdoctor named Tzamaranda Nychapi to Germany in order to purify the stadiums where the South American side would be playing. Was it any coincidence that they unexpectedly progressed to the second round, where they were narrowly beaten by England?

⚓ HAIR TONIC ⚓

Prior to his team's game against Switzerland in 2006, Brazil star Ronaldinho donated two locks of his hair for an auction organised by a Swiss newspaper to raise money for a cancer charity.

⊥ TOGO OR NOT TO GO ⊥

It was once the case that playing in the World Cup finals was the pinnacle of any player's career, one that they would do for free if asked. Not so with the players of Togo, who demanded 155,000 euros each to appear in Germany in 2006. When the Togolese FA told them to get lost, the players announced they were going on strike. This was all too much for manager Otto Pfister, who quit in disgust having managed to get the team to their first ever finals. He returned when the dispute was finally resolved on the eve of the tournament – and watched his team of overpaid superstars lose all three group games.

⊥ A MISS THAT LED TO A HIT? ⊥

There have been many explanations for Zinedine Zidane's crazy headbutt on Italy's Marco Materazzi in the 110th minute of the 2006 Final. Some commentators believe it has a lot to do with the French maestro's bullet header six minutes earlier that was amazingly tipped over the bar by Gianluigi Buffon. Not only would the goal have surely won the World Cup for France, but it would have been the most career goals scored by a player in World Cup finals (four), the most number of headed goals (four) and the most scored by a captain (two). In the event he at least claimed one record – the first player to be sent off in extra time of a World Cup final.

⊥ ON THE MONEY ⊥

In 2008, journalist Declan Hill claimed that four of the 2006 World Cup Finals matches were fixed by an Asian betting syndicate based in Bangkok. Among the matches allegedly affected were the clashes between Ghana and Italy in the group stages, Ghana and Brazil in the round of 16, and Ukraine versus Italy in the quarter final. Stephen Appiah, the Ghana captain, later confirmed that he had been targeted by match-fixers, although the team bosses have stridently refuted the allegations.

⚓ HANDY MILAN ⚓

There is no doubting the handiest player at the 2006 World Cup. Serbia and Montenegro's Milan Dudic deliberately handled the ball in the box on two occasions during his team's match against the Ivory Coast. He was sent off, Ivory Coast scored both penalties, and Serbia and Montenegro lost the match 3-2.

⚓ POISON PEN FOR SVEN ⚓

Blame for England's lamentable performance at the 2006 World Cup was laid firmly at the door of manager Sven-Göran Eriksson – at least by members of the press, who were nothing less than scathing in their verdict of the Swede's stewardship.

"We've sold our birthright down the fjord to a nation of seven million skiers and hammer throwers who spend half their lives in darkness" – *Daily Mail* hack Jeff Powell.

And there were more vitriolic hacks queueing up to pour scorn on poor Sven:

"This is the man who turned the golden generation into base metal, whose bedroom formations were far more adventurous than his footballing ones, who took us all for a ride but never had any idea where he was going." – Martin Lipton of the *Daily Mirror*.

"Sven-Göran Eriksson has been a £25m waste of money. An international fraud." – Brian Woolnough, *Daily Star*.

⚓ KEGS FOR WAGS ⚓

England's players might have flopped on the pitch, but the presence of their WAGs was a cause for celebration in the base camp town of Baden-Baden. Tortora Carmine, owner of the popular Garibaldi bar in the town, ordered an extra five kegs of lager to quench the ladies' thirst.

⚵ WHO'S WHO IN THE WAGS ⚵

While England's players struggled on the pitch, back at the team base in Baden-Baden, the efforts of their wives and girlfriends (WAGs) to outdo each other in the publicity stakes were of world championship quality. The main protagonists were:

Victoria Beckham, wife of former England captain David.
Cheryl Tweedy, singer in Girls Aloud and girlfriend (now wife) of defender Ashley Cole.
Coleen McLoughlin, girlfriend (now wife) of Wayne Rooney.
Carly Zucker, fitness instructor, wife of Joe Cole.
Melanie Slade, then an A-level student and girlfriend of 17-year-old wunderkind Theo Walcott.
Elen Rives, former waitress and fiancée of Frank Lampard.
Nancy Dell'Olio, girlfriend of manager Sven-Göran Eriksson.

⚵ WHO NEEDS TICKETS? ⚵

More than 70,000 England fans poured into Stuttgart for the second round match against Ecuador. Just under 40,000 managed to get tickets to watch the match live – but with touts selling them at over £1,000, it's hardly surprising.

⚵ ONLY HERE FOR THE BEER ⚵

England might have slumped out of the 2006 World Cup at the hands of Portugal, but the thousands of fans at the AufSchalke Arena in Gelsenkirchen were at least able to drown their sorrows. The stadium's catering areas were connected to a 5km long beer-line, supplying roughly 52,000 litres of beer before, during and after the match.

⚵ NOT BAD FOR A FAT LAD ⚵

The 2006 tournament was Brazil striker Ronaldo's fourth. Despite rumours that he was past his best, he still managed become the tournament's all-time highest scorer, scoring three to reach a total of 15 and surpassing West German Gerd Müller's long-standing record of 14.

⚐ POSTCARD FROM HOME ⚐

All 23 players in the Ivory Coast squad in 2006 were foreign-based. Indeed, only one player, the goalkeeper Jean-Jacques Tizie, played his club football outside Europe. The individual players' respective teams at the time were as follows:

1 GK Jean-Jacques Tizie – (Esperance, TUN)
2 MF Kanga Akale – (Auxerre, FRA)
3 DF Arthur Boka – (Strasbourg, FRA)
4 DF Kolo Toure – (Arsenal, ENG)
5 MF Didier Zokora – (Saint-Etienne, FRA)
6 DF Blaise Kouassi – (Troyes, FRA)
7 MF Emerse Fae – (Nantes, FRA)
8 FW Bonaventure Kalou – (Paris St-Germain, FRA)
9 FW Arouna Kone – (PSV Eindhoven, NED)
10 MF Gilles Yapi Yapo – (Young Boys, SUI)
11 FW Didier Drogba – (Chelsea, ENG)
12 DF Abdoulaye Meite – (Marseille, FRA)
13 DF Marc Zoro – (Messina, ITA)
14 FW Bakary Kone – (Nice, FRA)
15 FW Aruna Dindane – (Lens, FRA)
16 GK Gerard Gnanhouan – (Montpellier, FRA)
17 DF Cyrille Domoraud – (Creteil, FRA)
18 MF Kader Keita – (Lille, FRA)
19 MF Yaya Toure – (Olympiakos, GRE)
20 MF Guy Demel – (Hamburger SV, GER)
21 DF Emmanuel Eboue – (Arsenal, ENG)
22 MF Romaric – (Le Mans, FRA)
23 GK Boubacar Barry – (Beveren, BEL)

⚐ SUN PUTS ROOF TECHNOLOGY IN THE SHADE ⚐

The German football authorities were understandably proud of the retractable roofs over their World Cup stadiums at Frankfurt and Gelsenkirchen. However bright sunshine streaming onto the pitches was not everyone's cup of tea. TV broadcasters in particular were peeved that the inevitable shadows late in the game were proving annoying to their viewers and suggested that the stadium roofs should be shut. FIFA, thankfully, took the players' best interests at heart for once and decided a few shadows were a less distressing sight than 22 footballers suffocating in the heat.

⚓ TYROS ⚓

Youngest squad at the 2006 World Cup: Ghana (average age 24 years and three months).

⚓ HEADLINE GRABBERS ⚓

England
Algeria
Slovenia
Yanks
The Sun newspaper gives its verdict on England's Group C draw for the 2010 Finals.

⚓ TV TRIUMPH ⚓

The 2006 World Cup was the biggest television event in history, watched by an estimated 26.29 billion viewers. The final itself attracted an estimated global audience of 715.1 million people.

⚓ EUROPEAN CUP ⚓

The 2006 tournament was the first World Cup with three Portuguese-speaking national football teams, namely Portugal, Brazil and Angola. It also first featured the first all-European semi-finals since the finals of 1982.

⚓ WHEELER DEALING ⚓

Hosting a World Cup is big business, and the successful applicant knows that it will bring huge economic benefits. Which is why the four-yearly bunfight to secure the bid is often rife with accusations of underhand dealing. On the eve of the vote to decide the 2006 venue, German satirical magazine Titanic decided to exploit this by sending letters to all the FIFA representatives, offering gifts in exchange for votes for Germany. It was, of course, an elaborate spoof – but such was the resulting firestorm of controversy when Germany got the nod, there were even calls for a re-vote.

⚓ DEMPSEY DUCKS OUT ⚓

Then there was the curious case of FIFA Oceania delegate Charles Dempsey. Instructed by his home federation to vote for South Africa, Dempsey suddenly abstained altogether, citing "intolerable pressure" on the eve of the vote. Had he voted as originally instructed, the count would have been a 12–12 tie. FIFA president Sepp Blatter, who favoured the South African bid, would have had to cast the deciding vote.

⚓ WHAT'S IN A NAME? ⚓

Such is the power of the World Cup sponsors, FIFA will do anything to ensure they get things their way. That includes riding roughshod over any existing sponsorship deals the host country might have arranged. In Germany, this even included renaming stadiums in case they should offend the moneymen. For example the Allianz Arena in Munich was reinvented as the FIFA World Cup Stadium, Munich for the duration of the tournament, and any company logo or mention of the Allianz firm was erased from the ground and its surroundings.

⚓ LOW-SCORING GOAL CHAMP ⚓

When Germany's Miroslav Klose claimed the Golden Boot as top scorer in 2006, his five goals was the lowest total to win the prize since 1962.

⚓ TEAM GAME ⚓

No player from the winning Italian squad scored more than two goals during the 2006 tournament – though ten different players had scored for the team, tying the record for the most goalscorers from any one team.

⚑ A CASCADE OF CARDS ⚑

There might not have been many goals, but there were red and yellow cards in abundance. Indeed the 2006 tournament easily surpassed the unenviable record for cards held by the 1998 event. Players received a total of 345 yellow cards and 28 red cards, with Russian referee Valentin Ivanov handing out 16 yellow and four red cards in the second round match between Portugal and Holland.

⚑ THE BATTLE OF NUREMBERG ⚑

In every World Cup there is a match that makes up for a lack of goals with a surfeit of punches, fouls and red cards. The 2006 tournament was no exception, thanks to the infamous Battle of Nuremberg between Portugal and Holland on June 25. On paper two of the competition's most attractive and talented sides, their second round clash had been eagerly anticipated by football purists. Instead it turned into an ugly free-for-all in which cards were distributed like confetti, four players were sent off, and a record-breaking 16 booked. The trouble started after just eight minutes when Holland's Boulahrouz was booked for a foul on Ronaldo. This was the catalyst for 90 minutes of cynical foul and counter foul, resulting in early baths for Boulahrouz and van Bronckhorst of Holland, Deco and Costinha of Portugal. Indeed the mayhem was interrupted only once, in the 23rd minute, when Maniche of Portugal scored the decisive goal of the game.

⚑ THE GOSPEL ACCORDING TO BIG PHIL ⚑

"Jesus Christ may be able to turn the other cheek, but Luis Figo is not Jesus Christ." – Portugal manager "Big" Phil Scolari offers his take on Figo's decision to headbutt Holland's Giovanni van Brockhorst during the infamous Battle of Nuremberg.

⚓ SWISS CHEESED OFF ⚓

England have long been the butt of jokes about their inability to win penalty shoot-outs – but they have a long way to go to be as bad as the hapless Swiss. During a yawn-inducing goalless group match against Ukraine in 2006, Switzerland failed to score any of their three shoot-out penalties, the first team ever to do so. They also became the first team to be eliminated from the World Cup without conceding any goals. Mind you, apart from that their only defeat in 24 World Cup games, including qualifiers, was at home to Luxembourg.

⚓ A MASCOT CALLED ZAKUMI ⚓

The official mascot for the 2010 FIFA World Cup is a leopard called Zakumi . His name comes from "ZA", the international abbreviation for South Africa, and "kumi", a word that means "ten" in various African languages (2010, geddit?). The mascot's colours reflect those of the host nation's playing strip – yellow and green.

⚓ GERMAN HEX ⚓

England might have beaten them in 1966, but Germany/West Germany have progressed further than the three lions in each of the 10 successive tournaments, and have won the Cup twice.

⚓ THE BEST FANS IN THE WORLD? ⚓

Mexico, managed for most of their campaign by Sven-Göran Eriksson, very nearly failed to qualify for the 2010 tournament after losing three of their first four matches. This calamitous form did not stop an average of 81,600 fans watching each of their home matches – including 104,000 for the match against the USA – the highest among the finalists.

⚑ LONG HAUL FOR URUGUAY ⚑

Uruguay played 20 qualifying matches, including a two-leg playoff against Costa Rica, the most of any teams in South Africa this year.

⚑ SIGN OF THE SIX ⚑

At Euro 2000, Yugoslavia let in six goals against Holland. Six years later, as Serbia and Montenegro, they conceded six against Argentina. At World Cup 2010 they will be known as plain old Serbia – but will it stop another thrashing? Germany, Australia and Ghana, the other teams in Group D, will be licking their lips.

⚑ GHANA'S SERB CONNECTION ⚑

Ghana have been coached by three Serbs in the last 10 years: Ratomir Dujkovic, Milan Živadinovic, and now Milovan Rajevac.

⚑ STADIUM ROUND-UP ⚑

Here's a run-down of the stadiums that will be used in the 2010 World Cup Finals in South Africa.

NAME	CITY	CAPACITY	ALTITUDE
Green Point Stadium	Cape Town	70,000	Sea level
Moses Mabhina	Durban	70,000	Sea level
Ellis Park	Johannesburg	61,000	1,753m
Vodacom Park	Bloemfontein	48,000	1,400m
Nelson Mandela Bay	Port Elizabeth	48,000	Sea level
Royal Bafokeng	Rustenburg	42,000	1,500m
Loftus Versfeld	Pretoria	50,000	1,214m
Mbombela	Nelspruit	46,000	660m
Peter Mokaba	Polokwane	46,000	1,310m
Soccer City	Johannesburg	94,700	1,753m

⚑ THE BIG AND THE SMALL OF IT ⚑

As well as England, Group C contains the biggest (USA) and smallest (Slovenia) competing nations in this year's World Cup.

⚓ IT'S THAT MAN AGAIN ⚓

Algeria coach Rabah Saâdane knows the job inside out.
He should do – this is his fifth stint in charge of the
national team since 1996.

⚓ THE GROUPS ⚓

The draw for the group stage of the 2010 World Cup were made on
December 4 2009 and produced the following match-ups.

GROUP A: South Africa, Mexico, Uruguay, France
GROUP B: Argentina, Nigeria, South Korea, Greece
GROUP C: England, United States, Algeria, Slovenia
GROUP D: Germany, Australia, Serbia, Ghana
GROUP E: Holland, Denmark, Japan, Cameroon.
GROUP F: Italy, Paraguay, New Zealand, Slovakia
GROUP G: Brazil, North Korea, Ivory Coast, Portugal
GROUP H: Spain, Switzerland, Honduras, Chile

Notable absentees are Russia, who lost out in the UEFA play-offs to
relative minnows Slovenia, and African champions Egypt, who were
defeated by maghreb rivals Algeria in a tense play-off decider. Other
national teams with considerable football pedigrees, such as Sweden,
Croatia and the Czech Republic also failed to make it through the
qualifying group stages.

⚓ A MATCH TO FEAR ⚓

This year is the first that North Korea have appeared at
the World Cup finals since their heroic efforts in 1966,
when they beat Italy. Much has changed since, not least
politically – and there is the chance of a potentially
stormy clash with South Korea. However as they could
only possibly meet in the final or the third place play-off,
the Koreas would have to reach the semi-finals first.

⚓ FIRST PAST THE POST ⚓

The first team to qualify for the 2010 World Cup – apart of
course from the hosts South Africa – was Japan, when they beat
Uzbekistan on June 6 2009.

⚓ REGULAR UNDERDOGS ⚓

They may be regarded as minnows, but Cameroon have qualified for six of the last eight World Cups – that's one more than Holland, and two more than Portugal or England.

⚓ THE CURSE OF THE CHAMPIONS ⚓

Italy, as reigning champions, will be among the favourites in 2010. But should they be? Apart from Brazil in 1962, no holders have ever managed to retain the trophy.

⚓ SPICY CHILEANS ⚓

Chile amassed an impressive seven red cards during their qualifying games for the 2010 tournament – Cristian Alvarez was sent off in the first match against Argentina, then Jorge Valdivia saw red in the seventh fixture against Brazil, Ismael Fuentes and Gonzalo Jara in the ninth qualifying match against Ecuador, Mauricio Isla in the twelfth fixture against Uruguay, Alexis Sanchez in the return fixture against Brazil (Chile's sixteenth match), and then finally Fabian Orellana in the penultimate qualifying game against Colombia. Despite such a poor disciplinary record their results were good enough to ensure a second place finish behind group winners Brazil in the CONMEBOL table, thus securing automatic qualification along with Brazil, Paraguay and Argentina. Chile shouldn't have any problems playing with 10 or even 9 men come the 2010 tournament – they are more than acquainted with it.

Strangely, in the two matches against Peru, in which a traditionally fierce rivalry dating back to the War of the Pacific often rears its ugly head, there were no Chilean sendings-off, although Peruvian winger Juan Vargas did see red, and admittedly there were 8 yellow cards dealt out in each of the home and away matches.

Chile are forever associated with the red card, it seems – apart from their nickname, *la roja* (the red ones), Chile legend Carlos Caszely was the first player to be officially sent off with a red card during the 1974 World Cup, in a match against West Germany.

⚐ WELCOME BACK ⚐

Honduras, who have qualified for the 2010 tournament, last appeared in the World Cup finals in 1982, when they stunned the hosts Spain by scoring after only eight minutes hanging on for a hugely creditable 1-1 draw. They then went on to draw 1-1 with Northern Ireland before losing by a single 88th minute goal to Yugoslavia.

⚐ GOALSCORING SUPERPOWER ⚐

The USA come to the 2010 tournament as underdogs, but also having scored the most goals in qualifying. Their 43-goal haul was seven more than Mexico's tally of 36. Their biggest win came in an 8-0 hammering of Barbados, in which Fulham midfielder Clint Dempsey scored in the first minute.

⚐ WAYNE ON TARGET ⚐

England's Wayne Rooney found the net 10 times to become the top scorer in the qualifying stages for the 2010 World Cup Finals. Samuel Eto'o (9), Diego Forlan (7), and Tim Cahill (4) were also prolific for Cameroon, Uruguay, and Australia, respectively. Sympathy to Burkina Faso's Moumouni Dagano and Osea Vakatalesau of Fiji, who both bagged 12 goals but whose teams failed to qualify.

⚐ DM PREFERS PM ⚐

Argentina's national squad trained in the afternoon during the qualifiers – because head coach Maradona liked to get up at noon. It was hardly surprising that the bickering among players and coaching staff led to a revolving door policy where an astonishing 78 different players were called up in Maradona's first 10 months in charge, the most by any team on the road to South Africa.

⚖ GOALSHY KIWIS GET THROUGH ⚖

New Zealand progressed to their first finals in 28 years, despite scoring just 14 goals in qualifying – the lowest of any side in the 2010 Finals.

⚖ AFRICAN SHOWDOWN ⚖

Egypt and Algeria both finished with 13 points from six games and a goal difference of +5:

CAF Third Round Group C table – final standings

Team	Pld	W	D	L	GF	GA	GD	Pts
Algeria	6	4	1	1	9	4	+5	13
Egypt	6	4	1	1	9	4	+5	13
Zambia	6	1	2	3	2	5	–3	5
Rwanda	6	0	2	4	1	8	–7	2

The resulting winner-takes all playoff was played in neutral Sudan after near riots in both Cairo and Algiers. After a nerve-racking 90 minutes, the Algerians won the match 1-0 to qualify for the first time since 1986 – and will be in England's group in the Finals.

⚖ OLD HANDS ONLY ⚖

For the first time in the history of the World Cup, there are no debutants in the final 32 of the 2010 tournament.

FEET OF THE CHAMELEON
Ian Hawkey

Shortlisted for the William Hill Sports Book of the Year

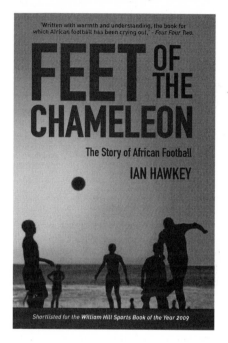

'THE BOOK FOR WHICH AFRICAN FOOTBALL HAS BEEN CRYING OUT'
FourFourTwo

'Perfectly timed ahead of next year's World Cup in South Africa,
Hawkey's study of the entire continent through football tackles a lot of
ground ... Hawkey's narrative will appeal as much to those interested in
the history and geography of Africa as it will to aficionados of the sport.'

Financial Times

Feet of the Chameleon is the compelling story of African football,
tracing the development of the world's favourite sport through the
turbulent social history of a fascinating continent.

Available at all good bookshops

The World Cup's Strangest Moments

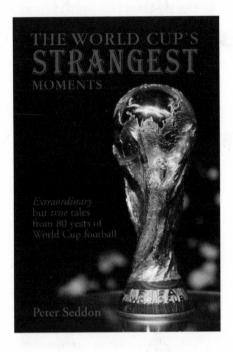

The World Cup's Strangest Moments is an entertaining collection of tales from every single tournament to date. It features spectacular failures, humiliating defeats, wonder goals, incompetent organisers, tragic accidents, supersubs, crazy 'keepers and much more, capturing the unforgettable moments of magic and misery that make the World Cup such a unique spectacle.

Paperback | 304pp | £8.99 | 9781906032913

Praise for Peter Seddon's football writing:

'The game is finally getting the literature it deserves.' *The Times*
'Brilliantly tackled…unique.' *London Evening Standard*
'Mightily impressed.' *When Saturday Comes*
'Exhaustively researched….fascinating.' *The Independent*

FRONT COVER

BACK COVER